Roger,
Thanks again for the opportunity
Love, Peace and Happy Reading!
Cha̶___

Life Is A Business!

Manage It Better So You'll Enjoy It More

---

9 Key Principles To A Prosperous Life

Charles E. Cox, Jr.

Life Is A Business! Publishing
St. Paul, Minnesota

Life Is A Business!
Manage It Better So You'll Enjoy It More
9 Key Principles To A Prosperous Life

Charles E. Cox, Jr.

Published by:
Life Is A Business! Publishing
P.O. Box 11767
St. Paul, Minnesota 55111

ISBN, paperback, revised ed.   978-1-4507-2943-7
ISBN, Amazon paper ed.   978-0-6155-9345-6
                                0-6155-9345-3 (ISBN-10)
ISBN, digital, revised ed.   978-1-4507-2946-8
ISBN, work book   978-1-4507-2947-5
ISBN, CD set   978-1-4507-2944-4

Printed in the United States of America.

Cover design by Derek Chiodo, www.ecovermakers.com
Edited by Susan M. Carter, www.authorsanonymous.com

Library of Congress Control Number: 2011925626

Disclaimer:

The purpose of this book is to educate and entertain. The author and Life Is A Business! Publishing shall have neither liability nor responsibility to any person or entity with respect to loss or damage caused, or alleged to have been caused, directly or indirectly, by the information contained in this book.

FORTUNE and FORTUNE 500 are trademarks of Time Inc., which are registered in the U.S. and in other countries. This book and its author is in no way affiliated with, or sponsored by, Time Inc. or Fortune magazine.

You Are on the Path to Prosperity When…

You've **realized** that your **life is a business** and through the **knowledge** you received by reading this book, your **thinking shifts** in a manner where you've become more **disciplined** in your **decision making** and **advocacy** for yourself and your family. Ultimately, you've become **empowered** to **purposefully** and **actively** navigate your life to **prosperity**.

Prosperity is the state of flourishing, thriving, success, or good fortune. Prosperity often encompasses wealth but also includes other factors which are independent of wealth to varying degrees, such as happiness and health.[1]

---

1 http://en.wikipedia.org/wiki/Prosperity

What This Book is Not

Too many of us chase the lifestyle and not the life itself – managing your life like a business requires a commitment to planning for and achieving success in all aspects of our lives.

Life Is A Business! is not another "get rich quick" book—there are enough of those types of books in print already. If you have purchased this book thinking this is one of them, take it back; you will be wasting your time and your money.

However, if you want to change your life for the better, improve your finances, and strengthen your relationships, you hold in your hands a blueprint for success. If you are willing to make a commitment to strategically plan for your life's success, then this book is a must read for you!

This book is dedicated to the memory of:

Kathleen "Katie" A. McWatt

and

Jeffrey R. Logan

February 8, 1931 – April 19, 2010

March 30, 1964 – January 31, 2009

Both of you touched my life,

in different ways,

and at different times,

but both in ways I've never forgotten.

Rest in Peace

Table of Contents

In The Beginning...

The Book's Origin

Life Is A Business! is the result of my personal poor life choices, bad business decisions, ultimate rebound and months of rigorous research and self-discovery. At the heart of the concept "life is a business, manage it better so you will enjoy it more" is a comparison of one's personal life and that of a Fortune 500[1] business to demonstrate how they closely mirror each other and are in many ways identical.

The Book's Purpose

This book is a life-improvement resource. Its purpose is to help you realize that managing your life is no different than managing a large corporation; to educate you by teaching you nine Key Principles and to move you to ACTION. To achieve a life filled with prosperity, you must start with action.

The Book's Intended Audience

This book is written for every person who currently resides on "Main Street" in any city, state or country; people who want to improve their lives and are willing to invest in themselves to accomplish success. This book can be used by life coaches to help

---

1 FORTUNE and FORTUNE 500 are trademarks of Time Inc., which are registered in the U.S. and in other countries. This book and its author is in no way affiliated with, or sponsored by, Time Inc. or Fortune magazine.

them teach individuals the importance of analyzing their lives as a whole to make relevant changes. Although not intended to be a business textbook, colleges and universities can use this book to challenge students to evaluate their lives and individual missions to become and remain productive citizens, leaders, future employees and entrepreneurs.

The Author's Frame of Reference

The term "Fortune 500" refers to an annual listing compiled by Fortune magazine of the top 500 public companies in the U.S., as ranked by sales, assets, earnings, and capitalization. This list ranks only public companies that have issued securities through an offering and are traded on the stock market. This list is important to a number of financial groups, but particularly to investors, who study the performance of these select companies. In addition, academic and business researchers look to these companies to learn about best practices in various industries and to discover the secrets to their business and financial success.

There are several characteristics that all Fortune 500 companies embody. Each Key Principle outlined in this book mirrors one or more of those characteristics. Hence, the interrelation between life and business.

Characteristics of a Fortune 500 Company:

1. Vision
2. Empowerment
3. Performance
4. Team Approach
5. Customer Service
6. Quality
7. Communication
8. Ethics
9. Wellness
10. Profit

Every decision we make in life is a business decision. Every decision has three possible outcomes:

1. **Positive Result** – increases, enhances or otherwise positively impacts your bottom line.
2. **Negative Result** – decreases, deflates or otherwise negatively impacts your bottom line.
3. **Future Positive or Negative Result** – impacts your bottom line in the future; not immediately measurable.

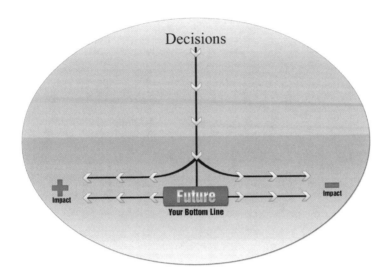

The Book's Organization

This book is organized into nine Key Principles, one per chapter. Each chapter begins by giving you an example of the language used in our personal lives and then the corporate equivalent, followed by a case study of a Fortune 500 corporation that exemplifies leadership using the Key Principle outlined in that chapter. The remaining chapter content shows how the principle transfers to our personal lives and teaches through discussion methods how to incorporate that principle into our daily lives.

11

The Author's Hopes

It's my hope to spark a paradigm shift across the world, a shift in the way we all view our lives. I also hope to lead and participate in a movement—a movement that will mobilize large groups of people to begin to live a life of prosperity.

Knowledge	Wealth	Prosperity	Movement
The fact or condition of knowing something with familiarity gained through experience or association	The condition of being successful or thriving; especially economic well-being	A state of health, happiness, and prospering; affluence, good fortune	The act or process of moving; especially : change of place or position or posture

Source: www.merriam-webster.com

Acknowledgments

I would like to extend a special thank you to my
self-publishing "Dream Team."

Ronald C. Buford
    Marketing & Advertisement Design, www.pr3e.com

Susan Carter
    Editor, www.authorsanonymous.com

Ryan T. Scott
    Public Relations, Phat & Skinny Consulting (Minneapolis, MN)

Rosalind R. Sullivan ESQ
    Writing Consultant, www.rsullivanlaw.com

Peter Whitcomb
    Illustrator, www.whitcombcreative.com

Overview of the 9 Key Principles to a Prosperous Life

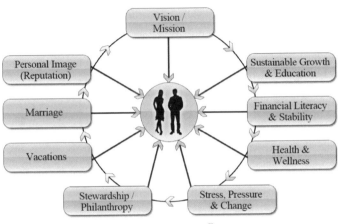

The Life Is A Business! (TM)
Blueprint To Prosperity

Key Principle #1: Vision/Mission

Create a clear vision of what you want for your life—it will pave a clear path to an attainable mission for action, giving your life purpose.

The lack of vision and mission almost always guarantees failure.

Key Principle #2: Sustainable Growth & Education

Keep strong, steady growth and a commitment to education at the forefront of your vision.

Accelerated growth without a strong foundation and sustainable long-term plan leads to chaos and erosion.

Key Principle #3: Financial Literacy & Stability

Commit to an ongoing quest to obtain and understand the truth about your finances so you can stabilize your financial health.

If you feel everyone is out to get your money, you are probably right.

Key Principle #4: Health & Wellness

Maintain a healthy mind, body and spirit.

Why work hard in life and not be able to enjoy it?

Key Principle #5: Stress, Pressure & Change

Prepare for inevitable stress, pressure and change so you can better manage your way through them.

*Stress, pressure and change happen in all of our lives —
you are not being singled out.*

Key Principle #6: Stewardship/Philanthropy

Serve your community to build a sense of community.

When you help others elevate their self-worth, you learn more than you teach.

Key Principle #7: Vacations

Plan and take vacations with your family.

*Every successful business person knows the importance of breaking away
from day-to-day routines. You and your family owe this to one another.*

Key Principle #8: Marriage

Enter marriage with the same caution and consideration as you would a business merger.

*Marriage is one of the biggest life decisions you will ever make —
treat it with the respect it deserves to set yourself up for success.*

Key Principle #9: Personal Image (Reputation)

Build an honorable personal and professional reputation.

*Your reputation can make or break your business — and your personal
relationships. It takes years to build and only seconds to destroy.*

Why I Wrote This Book and Why You Should Read It

Life is a Business!

What does that mean? It means just what I said: your life is a business. Furthermore, you are the CEO of your life and nearly every decision you make is a *business decision.*

Corporate CEOs are careful to make calculated decisions in business, yet many people — including those same CEOs — go through life making important personal decisions purely on emotion. Decisions made this way make us vulnerable to the world's predators; decisions made this way doom us to repeat costly mistakes; decisions made this way keep us in peril.

I know these things to be true because this is exactly how I made my decisions. And, guess what? I became vulnerable to the world's predators, repeated costly mistakes, and kept my life — and my family's life — in peril.

As tough as it is to admit, the inspiration for "Life Is a Business! Manage It Better So You'll Enjoy It More" didn't come from my success — it came from my failure.

Throughout the course of my life, I have had good luck and bad luck. I sometimes worked hard for little gain and sometimes gained much for little work. The fact is that I have experienced the highest of highs and the lowest of lows.

I spent little time organizing or focusing on my personal life. I haphazardly balanced my checkbook and chose to approximate the household budget in my head, never taking the time to actually put numbers to paper. I made poor purchasing decisions and stuffed receipts into my shirt pockets, later to be transferred to a random drawer or shoebox, making for a sloppy household accounting system. I gave little thought to building relationships with my family or examining who I invited into my circle of friends. I let my life lead me "wherever" without much planning or thought instead of me leading my life where I wanted it to go.

In business, I excelled. I amassed more than $4 million in real estate. I lived in a gated community, invested in rental properties and bought whatever I wanted, whenever I wanted it. I thought nothing of sauntering into a jewelry store, pointing into the shiny glass-protected case, and exchanging a few thousand dollars for a wristwatch — all in the span of a few minutes. I believed I was on top of the world and still climbing. I felt like I was unstoppable; doing everything right.

But, in fact, I was doing everything wrong.

My business was built on a house of cards, run much like I was running my life — haphazardly with no specific direction or forethought. By the time I realized I was doing it all wrong, the flimsy foundation collapsed and it was too late. The only thing I had really been successful at was systematically destroying my business. I used my credit irresponsibly and continually made knee-jerk buying decisions. I had no formal accounting system, the business grew at an unsustainable rate, and I repeatedly made bad business decisions. I refused to anticipate consequences of my actions and, as a result, bankrupted my corporation.

I fell, and I fell fast and hard.

Once the dust settled — after the home in the gated community was gone, the cars repossessed, credit cards defaulted on, foreclosure on my rental properties, and bank account wiped out — I began to reflect on my actions. Oblivious to how I'd earned my fate, I kept asking myself, "What did I do wrong?"

The answers came to me at a snail's pace. It took years to examine the ruins of both my personal and professional life as I desperately tried to sort it all out. But clarity did come.

As I examined the mechanics of my rollercoaster life, picking through the rubble and ashes of my newly shattered existence, I expected to have a slow, seeping, gradual realization of what to do differently wash over me. Instead, the gem of wisdom I was waiting for came in one quick flash — like being hit in the head with a 90-mile-an-hour fast ball:

"I need to manage my life like the business that it is."

My eye-opening discovery made perfect sense. How we run our lives mirrors how CEOs run businesses. Like CEOs, we need to pay attention to financials, nurture and respect good relationships, eliminate the negative ones, and become good problem solvers.

Like CEOs, we must understand the importance of stakeholders — the various people and groups that have an interest in the entity. In business, this circle of influencers and investors consists of owners, stockholders, customers, employees and their families, and the community. In your personal life, stakeholders include your spouse, your children, your co-workers, your employer, your friends, and members of community organizations. The wants and needs of each stakeholder are interrelated yet often contradictory and the business (you) must strive to maintain a balance.

Like CEOs, we have to look to the future and plan for it. And we have to pay attention to the details — when we take care of the small things, the big things practically take care of themselves.

As I contemplated my new view of life management, I realized that even the government acknowledges us as tiny, individual entities — businesses — when we are born. At birth we become, in essence, incorporated! How?

Think about it.

Our parents give us a name, have it officially recorded, and the government grants us a unique, one-of-a-kind, nine-digit Tax Identification Number (TIN), also known as our Social Security Number. This number is issued by the Internal Revenue Service (IRS) and its primary function is to track individuals for *taxation* purposes.

When a business is started, the owner gives it a name, has it officially recorded, and the government assigns an Employer Identification Number (EIN). This number is also a one-of-a-kind, nine-digit identifier used for *taxation* purposes.

Are you starting to see the resemblance between a Fortune 500 business and your business called LIFE?

The more I dissected the anatomy of a good business, the more I began to realize how my life could change for the better if I conducted my personal "business" the same way a corporate CEO conducts a successful operation.

I studied everything I could get my hands on about corporate giants of the industry... the Fortune 500 elite. I identified parallels between business management and life management and soon felt as though I had finally unlocked the mystery to reprogramming my rollercoaster life.

I changed my perspective—and it changed me. I began to carve out a new and enriched future for myself and my family.

Success comes with making good decisions

In the early years of life, most of us begin making business decisions long before we realize we are making them. Think back to the first time a parent gave you an allowance, or Grandma Tillie tucked $10 into your birthday card. Did you save it? Did you spend it? Did you save half and spend half? Did you give it away to charity? Did you "invest" it in a bag of lemons and a pound of sugar to "manufacture" lemonade to sell to the neighbors so you could double or triple your investment? Those are all business decisions you made in your very young life.

In the most recent presidential campaign of 2008 it was said over and over that "small business" is the back-bone of America. I couldn't agree more, but I view small business as more than a new startup or the place where millions of Americans commute to work every day. I view each and every one of us as an individual small business, with the potential to grow into a large, very successful and respected business; a business that will allow us to live and manage a life of prosperity.

The rebuilding and growth of America's financial markets, as well as our personal lives, rely heavily on us being great business operators. America will need us to be more vigilant regarding our finances than ever before. That means we *must* learn to make good decisions.

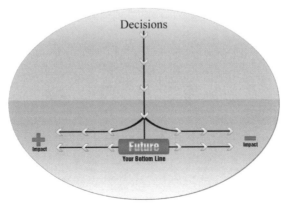

A business decision in a life of prosperity is defined as: **any decision you make that has a financial impact; an impact on your bottom line.** In other words: Follow the Money!

Your decisions can have a **positive** impact on your bottom line, or they can have a **negative** impact on your bottom line.

For example, paying cash when you make a purchase has a **positive** impact on your bottom line. By paying cash, you avoid getting caught in monthly payment cycles where you are charged often exorbitant interest rates. Paying cash also thwarts the possibility of being charged a late fee that triggers an increase to even higher interest rates as punishment for your tardiness.

The **decision** to pay your utility bill late is a business **decision** that has a *negative* impact on your bottom line. Nearly all creditors charge a "late fee" when bills are paid after the due date. This late fee payment negatively impacts your bottom line. And, if you habitually pay late, that **decision** will affect your credit score—a precious number that determines your creditworthiness when you attempt to finance a car or home. A damaged credit score will cost you hundreds—maybe thousands—of dollars more for your purchase.

The secret to tipping the scales of good decision-making in your favor is to simplify! Adopt basic principles and turn them into habits. Follow a proven path to life's rewards. Emulate success by running your life the way successful CEOs run their businesses.

Successful business people:
- seek outside advice
- recognize and admit their limitations
- exhibit passion for what they do in their business and personal lives
- recognize and accept the value of their business and themselves
- define and trust what they believe is their purpose in business and life
- visualize and focus on positive outcomes in their business and their life

- maintain a work and personal life balance
- develop and maintain a support system of people with similar mindsets
- maintain a level of self-confidence about their business and personal plans and actions
- maintain a keen awareness of their vision, mission and goals for their business and their lives

I have good news, and I have great news.

The good news is that learning to run your life like a business is not hard. It requires a new way of thinking and you must be willing to develop new habits, but it is doable and the reward is worth the effort.

The great news is that I've already done the hard work for you. I've studied "the masters" of industry, distilled the lessons learned into a simplified process, and packaged those lessons into nine key principles for a successful life — your prosperous life. If you do the exercises in this book and apply the principles, you will be well on your way to building your own stepping stones to success.

My life has changed and so can yours. It all begins by turning the page and getting started.

Chapter 1

Key Principle #1

Vision / Mission

ᔥ ᔥ

Vision/Mission for Our Lives/Passion

=

Vision/Mission Statement

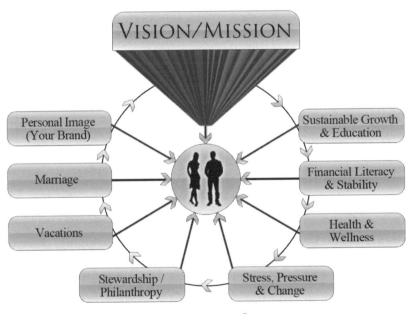

The Life Is A Business! ™
Blueprint To Prosperity

"Vision without action is a daydream.
Action without vision is a nightmare."

—Japanese Proverb

Case Study

General Electric

General Electric CEO:	Jeffrey Immelt
Number of Employees:	304,000
Fortune 500 Ranking:	#4
Industry:	Conglomerate
Location:	Fairfield, CT
Annual Revenue:	$156.7B

From turbines to TV, from household appliances to power plants, General Electric (GE) is plugged into businesses that have shaped the modern world. The company produces — take a deep breath — aircraft engines, locomotives and other transportation equipment, kitchen and laundry appliances, lighting, electric distribution and control equipment, generators and turbines, and medical imaging equipment. GE is also one of the preeminent U.S. financial services providers. GE Capital, comprising commercial finance, commercial aircraft leasing, real estate, and energy financial services, is its largest segment. GE's other segments are Energy, Technology Infrastructure, NBC Universal, and GE Home & Business Solutions.[1]

---

1 www.hoovers.com

❧ The Windows to Your Future ❧

If you think that having a vision and mission is too corporate and too complicated, think again. Visionaries—in business and in life—are leaders. They look ahead and make a choice to actively shape their own futures, framed in the present and fueled by passion. During his presidency, John F. Kennedy vowed to put a man on the moon—that's vision. Martin Luther King, Jr. "had a dream" that was destined to change the world—that's vision. Defining what your life or business will look like a year, two years, or five years from now—that's vision.

Your mission is the driving force, the compass, and the guide to realize your vision. Your mission is steeped in value and principle that set the standards and direction for realizing your vision's goals.

Together, the vision and mission become the windows to your future.

Vision and Mission Defined

Let's take a by-the-book look at the definitions for a vision statement and a mission statement.

A **vision statement** is sometimes referred to as a picture of the company in the future—what you think it will "look like;" it is the business inspiration for being in business, and the framework for strategic planning of the business. A vision statement describes the future of a company, where it wants to go and what it wants to be in the future.

Every great company establishes a vision for the company. Why? Because this vision drives the decisions made for the company. If decisions become contrary to the vision, either the vision needs to be re-evaluated or the actions need to be brought into alignment with the vision.

27

A **mission statement** is a formal, short, written statement of the purpose of a company or organization. The mission statement guides the actions of the organization, spells out its overall goal, provides a sense of direction, and influences decision-making. It provides "the framework or context within which the company's strategies are formulated."[1]

In the world of business, the terms "vision" and "mission" are often used interchangeably. However, a vision is typically associated with the broader view of the company — the big picture. The mission expresses the specific goals of the company and contains phrases aligned to the type of business or services provided by the business.

So what can we learn about vision and mission from GE, my case study subject?

I selected GE as the Fortune 500 Company to profile in this section because of its unique commitment to vision and instilling vision in its employees. According to an article in Soundview Executive Book Summaries, referencing the book, *"Jack Welch and the GE Way,"* authored by Robert Slater, Jack Welch, CEO of GE, required every employee to carry a wallet-sized card titled "Value Guides." The card reads:

> "Life is a trip worth taking, if you have the right travel agent—You!"
> —Rosalind R. Sullivan

GE Leaders...always with unyielding integrity:
- Have a passion for excellence and hate bureaucracy
- Are open to ideas from anywhere... and committed to Work-Out
- Live quality... and drive cost and speed for competitive advantage
- Have self confidence to involve everyone and behave in a boundaryless fashion
- Create a clear, simple, reality-based vision... and communicate it to all constituents
- Have enormous energy and the ability to energize others

---

1 http://en.wikipedia.org/wiki/

- Stretch... set aggressive goals... reward progress... yet understand accountability and commitment
- See change as opportunity... not threat
- Have global brains... and build diverse and global terms

Jack Welch is quoted as saying "I don't *run* GE, I *lead* GE." This statement reflects his assertion that good leaders inspire employees by creating a vision of how things can be done better.

Benefits of Having a Vision and Mission

Does a company need a vision and mission statement to function? The answer is, "Probably not." Yet, I doubt it is a coincidence that every Fortune 500 Company has both. It is clear from the GE example that articulated vision and mission statements are crucial to the success of any business. I wholeheartedly recommend that every person and household have both.

What's the benefit?

Creating your life's vision and mission statement will provide a solid foundation, impenetrable focus, and a natural flow for decisions. With a basic sense of direction in place, we approach decision-making with a sense of calm rather than chaos, particularly when things happen unexpectedly or when we're under a great deal of pressure.

> "A man to carry on a successful business must have imagination. He must see things as in a vision, a dream or the whole thing."
> —Charles M. Schwab

A vision and mission set the stage for companies to thrive rather than merely survive. Aligning efforts with an agreed-upon focus saves both time and frustration, and it makes a company much more profitable.

If these two seemingly boring and unobtrusive statements can have such an impact on business, think about the impact they can have on your life!

Instead of "going with the flow," you *direct* the flow.

Instead of passively reacting to what goes on around you, you actually *influence* what goes on around you.

Having a vision allows you to look at life's "big picture" and having a mission allows you to establish a plan of action based on that vision. You become the leader of your life, not just a bystander waiting idly away for the next big wave. I know what it is like to get swept away. At one point in my pseudo-successful business life, I was part owner of a real estate company and a sports bar, owner of a construction company, owned nearly 50 rental properties and attempted to maintain dual residency in both Minnesota and Nevada. This is the epitome of a blurred vision.

My justification for this life was that I *wanted* to do it. I thought I *could* do it. My decisions had nothing to do with an articulated vision. It did not make sense for me to own a sports bar with no prior restaurant experience. And, without a vision, I did not realize that the financial goal I was trying to reach could have been attained with far fewer properties and far less risk. My vision was blurred.

One might say that my vision was more than just blurred; I had no vision at all. Ironically, I was involved in creating the vision and mission statement for my real estate company. We as a business realized the importance of not only creating a vision and mission statement but having employee buy-in for carrying out the goals set out in the statements. To achieve that end, the statements were prominently displayed in the office for both employees and clients to see and were communicated verbally to employees. However, I still failed to understand the importance of having these statements for my personal life and keeping them "prominently displayed."

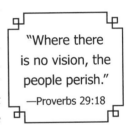

"Where there is no vision, the people perish."
—Proverbs 29:18

Without a clear vision, my mission was meaningless.

If you are still struggling to relate the idea of vision and mission statements to life, consider the non-business definition of vision:

"A vivid mental image;" "sight: the ability to see; the visual faculty; the perceptual experience of seeing; imagination: the formation of a mental image of something that is not

31

perceived as real and is not present to the senses; a religious or mystical experience of a supernatural appearance."[2]

Even in the non-business context, the concept of "vision" and "visualizing" is powerful. Creating a "vivid mental image," and using your imagination are encouraged when we are younger, but somehow fall to the wayside as we age. It is time to take back that power.

Still struggling to make sense of it all? Then replace the word "vision" with the word "passion." Our personal vision can also be described as our "passion" in life. If you are not passionate about life, you cannot live life to its fullest potential.

Encompassing the Bigger Picture

By now I hope I've convinced you that you need to create a vision statement and a mission statement for your life, and I'm going to walk you through the process of doing that at the end of this chapter. But before I do, I want to introduce one more concept related to your vision and mission statements that encompasses a broader perspective: If you are in a committed relationship, married, or have a family, it is important to create a vision and mission statement for the "bigger picture" that includes those relationships.

Although each individual in the relationship should have a vision statement, you should also have a vision statement for your long-term relationships.

<u>Committed Partnerships</u>

Whether you are considering marriage or not, creating a vision statement can be an outstanding exercise to strengthen a committed relationship. This process, though I recommend each person doing it alone, can be done in concert with your partner. You will follow the same instructions at the end of this chapter and agree upon a schedule for completion of the individual vision statements, which challenges both people to stay on task.

Once both of the individual vision statements are completed, the outcome can be shared. This type of information sharing is critical

---

2 Wordnetweb.princeton.edu/Perl/webwn

for continued growth individually and as a couple. When ignored, you set the stage for tumultuous relationships and avoidable misunderstandings.

Married Couples

Married couples have a much greater need for both a mission and vision statement. When two people (separate businesses) enter marriage (initiate a merger), it is extremely important and can be very worthwhile to compare and discuss individual statements. If one or both individuals have these statements, the process of creating and/or merging the two to create one vision should be significantly easier, and it paves the way for a well thought out mission statement. You are likely to uncover both minor and/or major differences that, when discussed early on, could help insure a more loving, productive union.

This is not to suggest that you do away with your individual vision and mission statements. However, if you compare your vision and mission statements and they seem very far apart or even inconsistent, you may want to have a candid heart-to-heart discussion with your spouse about how you plan to achieve your individual visions or follow your passion given the stark differences uncovered.

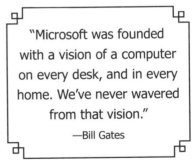

"Microsoft was founded with a vision of a computer on every desk, and in every home. We've never wavered from that vision."

—Bill Gates

For your Family

Family vision and mission statements are an absolute must for several reasons, including strengthening the family bond and demonstrating good life / business habits.

Kids develop habits early in life that they take with them into adulthood. Most of these habits come from watching and emulating their parents, including their sense of vision and mission. If parents have taken the time to develop vision and mission statements, the next important step is to make sure your children are familiar with them.

All family members who are old enough to understand should be made aware of the existence of these statements as well as having an understanding of the content.

Kids are also quite capable of writing their own, age-appropriate vision and mission statements. They, too, need goals and will benefit from identifying a set of standards that serve as the foundation to achieve those goals.

> "The world has the habit of making room for the man whose actions show that he knows where he is going."
>
> —Napoleon Hill

TIP: In Corporate America, the vision and mission statements are usually posted where employees can read them. This is a good idea for families as well. With these statements in plain sight your family is more likely to follow them. When children see their family following a planned path, they too, are likely to incorporate that type of organization into their lives, including school.

Write Your Vision and Mission Statement

Our personal success depends on how well we define and live by the vision we prepare for ourselves. Therefore, it is not an exercise to be taken lightly or completed quickly. Your vision and mission statements require thought, consideration, and contemplation.

Though typically consisting of a few succinct sentences, writing a vision statement is not a quick and easy task. We are forced to ask ourselves some difficult questions:

"Who am I?"

"What mark do I want to leave on this earth (my legacy)?"

"Where am I comfortable going and where should I never be seen?"

"What will I say and what will I never be heard saying?"

"What will I always do and what will I never do?"

Sounds simple, right? Yet, many of us never ask ourselves these value questions, and those of us who have, know how difficult it can be to arrive at truthful answers. It is my hope that your ideas about your vision take you much deeper in thought and self-examination.

Writing a mission statement is equally as important as identifying your vision. The mission statement is your life's road map. Would you plan to drive cross country without a road map or some sense of where you are going and how to get there? I doubt many of you would. So, why would you set out on this journey called life without a mission statement? With a well thought out vision statement in place, you should be able to prepare a mission statement with relative ease.

Your mission statement serves the same purpose for you that it serves every Fortune 500 Company. It is a constant reminder of how your vision will be achieved. Jack Welch the distinguished former CEO of GE Corporation has a great quote about good business leaders and vision:

"Good business leaders create a vision, articulate the vision, passionately own the vision, and relentlessly drive it to completion."

How to create a vision statement for your life

Step 1:   **Define who you are and what you want in life — identify your values.**

Remember to think of your vision as your passion.

What are you passionate about? Your passions are normally based in part on your values. Your values are the foundation of who you are or who you hope to become. It is very important to lay the foundation before drafting the vision statement; therefore this is the first action in Step 1.

Review the directives and questions on page 36, carefully formulate your thoughts, and write down your responses. Doing so will allow you to develop the framework for your vision and mission statement. Use the thought-provoking questions listed on page 34 to help jumpstart your answers. Take as much time as necessary to answer these questions completely before writing your vision statement.

- Identify your top ten values.
- Identify the ten things you most enjoy doing.
- Identify the ten things you least enjoy doing. (This is just as important in developing your vision statement.)
- What strengths and accomplishments in life have other people identified in you?
- When you retire from your current job, how would you want to spend your time?
- Identify three things you do in your life that leave you fulfilled.

Step 2:   **Identify your Goals.**

Using the information you uncover about yourself in Step 1, rephrase your desires and passion into goals, and define how your strengths will help you achieve your goals.

Developing goals is the beginning of establishing the components of your vision statement. Goals are what you want out of life, the things that you want to do based on the values and beliefs you outlined in Step 1.

Remember that your vision statement is future thinking so these goals should be very broad and long term, not small, easily and quickly achievable goals. You will prepare goals for the short term during the mission statement section.

Narrow your list to your top five (5) broad goals.

This step may take several drafts before you can come up with just five goals. However, remember the purpose of this section is to prepare a vision statement for your life that is succinct, clear and based on your value system, strengths and weaknesses.

Step 3:   **Uncover the real, human value in your goals.**

Step 3 is the connection between what is essentially brainstorming and the articulation of your vision. Articulating your goals is essential but it is crucial to determine the human value in your goals in order to establish your vision.

Here is an example. Let's say that you have identified the goals listed in the first column below. The second column identifies the "human values in your goals." Review the example carefully and notice the change in language and words used in the second column to describe the goals in the first column.

Goals from Step 2	Human Value
To teach adult learners full time	To empower and inspire, commitment to success
To create an organization focused on helping women live better lives	Compassion, service, community, healing, optimism
To spend my life communicating effectively in an effort to teach as many people as possible how to live debt free	Listening, teaching, compassion, future success, abundance
To retire at age 55	Allow time to give back to the community by volunteering, dedication, belief in service and sacrifice

Using this example as your guide, create a similar chart listing the goals that you have identified. Try to determine what values drive the goals/passions that you articulated in Step 2. We will use these values to turn these goals into a vision statement.

You MUST believe your vision statement! Writing something for the sake of writing something is futile and a waste of time. This step should help you to define the belief system behind your goals which will ultimately lead to your belief in your vision.

Step 4:   Formulate your vision statement.

Using the value words you developed in Step 3, combine your values and goals and write your vision statement. This may take some time. If you don't feel you have enough information to draft a vision statement, go back to Step 1 and redraft some of your responses. Also, you may have to spend more time with Step 3 to properly evaluate the values behind your passions.

Continue to revise and polish your words until you have a statement that inspires you, energizes you, and motivates you to achieve it. While there are no "rules" regarding the length of a vision statement, your finished statement should be approximately 50 words long. The point is to get to the core of your vision — what do you want to achieve?

To help you, here are a few examples of vision statements:

Company	Vision Statement
Apple	Apple is committed to bringing the best personal computing experience to students, educators, creative professionals and consumers around the world through its innovative hardware, software and Internet offerings.
Google	To develop a perfect search engine.
PepsiCo	PepsiCo's responsibility is to continually improve all aspects of the world in which we operate – environment, social, economic – creating a better tomorrow than today. Our vision is put into action through programs and a focus on environmental stewardship, activities to benefit society, and a commitment to build shareholder value by making PepsiCo a truly sustainable company.
Allegiance Real Estate Services (co-written by author)	Allegiance Real Estate Services is dedicated to the creation and demonstration of a new corporate concept of linked prosperity. Our mission consists of three interrelated pledges: Service Pledge • Provide a full range of Real Estate Services utilizing time proven methods , innovation and education to stay on the cutting edge of the real estate industry • Provide service with the highest standard of honesty, integrity and quality customer service Social Pledge • Embrace the unique needs of the multicultural environment of our communities, associates and clients Economic Pledge • Operate the company on a sound financial basis of sustaining profitable growth, increasing value for our shareholders and creating career opportunities and financial rewards for our employees • Establish economic security for our clients through real estate opportunities

Examples of Personal Vision Statements

Personal	Vision Statement
Training for an Olympic medal	"I stand on the top tier of the winners' platform to receive the Olympic Gold Medal for the 100 meter dash. I watch proudly as my country's flag is raised and sing along as my national anthem is played. I wave to the huge, cheering crowd."
Career goals	"I have graduated from a prestigious law school and been offered an associate position in a small, growing law firm where I will be offered a partnership in three years; I will give back to the community in which I live. I am blessed with great friends and a loving family."

How to create a Mission Statement for your life

Before drafting your mission statement, let's clarify the difference between a vision and a mission statement.

As stated earlier, a vision is typically associated with the broader view of the company — the big picture. The mission expresses the specific goals of the company and contains phrases aligned to the type of business or services provided by the business. For our personal Mission Statement we identify the goals we have set for our lives and how they will be carried out. It is important to note that a vision is something that is very broad and reflects motivation rather than practicality. Therefore, some vision statements you read may seem broad or even unattainable on the surface.

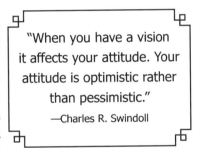

"When you have a vision it affects your attitude. Your attitude is optimistic rather than pessimistic."

—Charles R. Swindoll

In contrast, a Mission Statement should provide action steps that you can immediately apply to achieve your vision. Some of the steps may seem redundant. The vision and mission are so closely entwined that the creation of your mission statement will require the same thought process as creating your vision statement. Your Mission Statement has two distinct differences: (1) Action (2) Now.

In other words your Mission Statement adds Actions to carry out your vision and these actions are in the Now, or the very near future.

There are four steps to creating a Mission Statement for your life. The first three steps require answers to three critical questions:

Step 1:   **What is my life about (Purpose)?**

Answering this question is a necessary step to differentiate the unimportant wants and desires of life from your true calling or your genuine inspiration in life. You should have uncovered many of these answers in the previous vision writing exercise. Use this step to narrow the scope even further for your Mission Statement.

The goal of identifying your life's purpose is to create statements of action that will carry out your vision. Therefore, you must take the goals you just documented and turn them into action statements. For example, if you look at PepsiCo's vision and mission statement together you will see that the Mission Statement outlines specific action steps to achieve the vision.

Vision	Mission
"PepsiCo's responsibility is to continually improve all aspects of the world in which we operate - environment, social, economic - creating a better tomorrow than today."	Our mission is to be the world's **premier consumer products company** focused on **convenient foods and beverages**. We seek to **produce financial rewards to investors** as we **provide opportunities for growth and enrichment** to our **employees, our business partners and the communities** in which we operate. And in everything we do, we **strive for honesty, fairness and integrity.**

Notice that the Vision Statement does not mention beverages or vending. It basically states that PepsiCo wants to improve the world.

The mission states, in summary, that PepsiCo will achieve its vision by:
(1) becoming the premier consumer products company,
(2) focusing on convenient foods,
(3) producing financial rewards,
(4) operating with honesty, fairness and integrity.

Notice that these statements are action statements that carry out four goals in order to achieve the vision for PepsiCo. When drafting your purpose statements, align them carefully with your Vision Statement. You are essentially going back to Step 2 of the vision writing process by reviewing "how" you created your vision statement.

Step 2.   What do I stand for (Values)?

The questions you examined in creating your Vision Statement should be reviewed and rewritten here for reflection and clarity. Use your identified values to create action steps to further the realization of your values. Review the PepsiCo example. Notice how the values are actually stated in the Mission Statement: honesty, fairness and integrity. Not all Mission Statements will use value words, but it is important to outline your values prior to developing your Mission Statement.

Step 3.   What actions do I take to manifest my Purpose and my Values?

This may be the most important question to answer. Your mission is an outline of the steps you will take to carry out your vision. Therefore, Mission is synonymous with Action. These actions should lead to the accomplishment of your vision.

Your task is to transform your purpose and values into action statements. In this step, focus on narrowing your list. Using the results of your purpose and vision statements, eliminate redundancy by combining similar statements into one action statement. Continue

41

to refine goals until you have a set of action statements that would likely achieve your vision.

Step 4:   Draft your Mission Statement.

Use the action statements that you developed in Step 3 and rework them into three to five bullet points. Don't be discouraged if this drafting step takes longer than you expected.

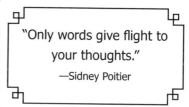
"Only words give flight to your thoughts."
—Sidney Poitier

Use these well-honed bullet points to write a paragraph using full sentences. This paragraph will be your Mission Statement. Remember that this first attempt to write your statement may not be your final draft. As you learn about the next 8 Key Principles, you may revisit both your vision and mission statements to make changes.

Your final Mission Statement will:
• Clearly express your vision
• Support your vision
• Be easy to understand
• Be tangible
• Be short enough for you to memorize or recall as needed
• Inspire and motivate you to action

Here are sample Mission Statements to jump start your efforts.

Corporate Mission Statement Examples

Company	Mission Statement
Walt Disney	The mission of The Walt Disney Company is to be one of the world's leading producers and providers of entertainment and information.
	Using our portfolio of brands to differentiate our content, services and consumer products, we seek to develop the most creative, innovative and profitable entertainment experiences and related products in the world.

Harley Davidson	We fulfill dreams through the experience of motorcycling, by providing to motorcyclists and to the general public an expanding line of motorcycles and branded products and services in selected market segments.

Personal Mission Statement Example

Anonymous Personal Mission Statement	"My mission is to champion others to grow personally, professionally, emotionally and spiritually by using my compassion, my unique perspective, and my belief in others' inherent goodness, integrity, and desire to achieve." -Anonymous

The final example shown above is a personal mission statement. To champion others is a mission that supports this person's belief (value) in the goodness of people. While the statement seems broad, one can tell from the mission statement that this person has made a decision in life to mentor, uplift or somehow represent people based on a value system that assumes that all people have some good in them that needs to be nurtured and supported. When writing your mission statement, include words that vividly describe the action you are going to take to fulfill your life's vision.

You have completed this chapter when you have a clear mission statement that drives your vision. Here is one more example of a properly executed vision and mission statement for Google.

Google Vision Statement	Google Mission Statement
To develop a perfect search engine.	Google's mission is to organize the world's information and make it universally accessible and useful.

First things first, don't get discouraged!

It may take several days or weeks of reviewing your answers before you can come up with a concise vision statement and a supporting mission statement for your life. Take your time. Remember that this statement will guide you through the rest of the chapters of this book and make it easier for you to apply the remaining 8 Principles to achieving your life of prosperity.

Stop. Breathe. Now pat yourself on the back. You have just completed the "heavy lifting" chapter of this book. You have set a foundation upon which you will build your life of prosperity.

Life is a business and nearly every decision in it is a business decision. Choosing to go through life without a vision/mission statement is a business decision that will negatively impact your bottom line. You will lose in the end.

The first key principle (the foundation) in establishing your life of prosperity is the creation of your vision / mission. Far too many of us continue walking through life blindly, repeating the same bad habits and wondering why we aren't getting the desired outcome. This problem is curable. We are all equipped with the ability to ask ourselves what we want for our lives; we are all equipped with skills to carry out our desires.

> "Nobody can go back and start a new beginning, but anyone can start today and make a new ending."
>
> —Maria Robinson

The process of creating a vision and mission statement can be tedious and therefore should not be rushed. Find a time and place where you are most relaxed to begin this work. For many, this exercise will represent the first step toward a paradigm shift—your transformation from one way of thinking to another. Be tenacious and don't procrastinate. Begin this process today.

Now that you have established the foundation of your life of prosperity, the next Key Principle, Strategic Planning and Education, will teach you to develop a strategy for living that life.

Vision
Mission
Goals
Value

❧ Key Principle #1 ❧

Vision/Mission

Create a clear vision of what you want for your life —
it will pave a clear path to an attainable mission for
action, giving your life purpose.

The lack of vision and mission almost always guarantees failure.

Chapter 2

Key Principle #2

Sustainable Growth & Education

Sustainable Growth & Education

=

Strategic Planning

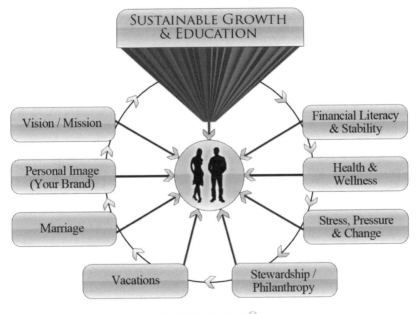

The Life Is A Business! ™
Blueprint To Prosperity

"Planning without action is futile, action without planning is fatal."

—Unknown

DuPont

DuPont CEO:	Ellen J. Kullman
Number of Employees:	58,000
Fortune 500 Ranking:	#86
Industry:	Chemicals
Location:	Wilomington, DE
Annual Revenue:	$26.1B

DuPont, a U.S. manufacturer of food, healthcare products, clothing, hardware and electronics, is ranked among the 50 largest U.S. industrial/service corporations by Fortune 500 magazine. In its 200-year history it has built up a staff of more than 85,000 people in 80 countries. DuPont owns more than 135 manufacturing and processing facilities, as well as 75 laboratories, and in 2009 it earned $26.1 billion in revenue.

DuPont's mission is to achieve "sustainable growth." This goal, defined as "increasing shareholder and societal value while decreasing the company's environmental footprint along the value chain in which we operate" has been DuPont's focus since shifting away from being primarily an explosives company in 1802. DuPont's own perception of sustainable business borrows from the Bruntland definition of sustainable development, and commits the company to "Implement those strategies that build successful businesses and achieve the greatest benefit for all stakeholders without compromising the ability of future generations to meet their needs."[1]

DuPont says its values and principles are non-negotiable. The company embraces safety, health, and environmental excellence; high standards of ethics and integrity in all business practices; and fair treatment of all the people associated with the company.[2]

---

1 http://en.wikipedia.org/wiki/Sustainable_development
2 www.hoovers.com

ᴄ⁓ Your Future's Foundation ⁓ᴐ

In the Introduction, I told you that the business I thought would sustain me through life was built "on a house of cards." My "building blocks" were thin, unsubstantiated assumptions, that didn't successfully support my business long term. Each decision I made was an independent action laid down in a catawampus fashion. I thought I had a knack for building wealth, fearlessly leading with my gut instincts. I also believed that if I just kept building, everything else would work itself out. Well, I learned the hard way that, when you build without a stable foundation, you compromise the integrity of the structure. I also soon realized that instincts are best developed with a healthy dose of knowledge—the more you know, the better your instincts.

A strong, stable business—and life—must have a solid foundation. You've taken the first step by establishing your vision and mission statements. Now it's time to put some action into those goals by creating a strategic plan for growth and fueling it with knowledge.

Controlled Business Growth

Let's first take a look at growth from the business perspective. Growth is a healthy, natural and desirable part of any business. However—and this is critical—it must be planned and controlled. Business growth should be financed by the profits that the business generates or by the capital that the owners invest in the company. On the riskier side of the scale, growth can also be financed by debt (borrowing/loans).

Business growth is typically marked with events such as a change in corporate structure, addition of employees, introduction of new products or services, or expansion through acquisition or establishing subsidiaries or branch offices. Without proper control, a company can either grow too fast—or not fast enough.

49

When a company grows too fast, it invests in equipment, products, and personnel, taking on huge amounts of debt. What seems like a financially sound decision to spark progress can quickly result in financial disaster. If the market doesn't embrace the changes made, the company is soon wallowing in a bottomless pit of debt from which it may never recover. Likewise, if a company doesn't grow quickly enough to meet market demand, it will lose its lifeblood for existence—customers.

> "Rule No. 1: Never lose money.
> Rule No. 2: Never forget Rule No. 1."
> —Warren Buffett

So, if the results are so unpredictable, how do businesses control the outcome?

Successful businesses control growth by developing a strategic plan.

Controlled Personal Growth

"How does growth apply to me as an individual?"

Great question, thanks for asking!

Think about all of the decisions you have made and will make that contribute to your life's "growth." Things like: buying a new car, boat, or house, investing in stocks and bonds, seeding a savings account, supporting a growing family, or starting a small business. These types of growth spurts are all tied to your financial ability to support them. Just as a business must take steps to control growth, so will you. Controlling growth makes it sustainable, and for growth to be sustainable it must be planned.

Here's an example of what that looks like.

Let's say you want to upgrade to a new, larger house. This is a growth decision for you and your family. The decision to buy a new home may be driven by any number of factors, including: emotion, desire, the need for more space, wanting to live up to the expectations of others, community, schools, or proximity to your job.

The first question you must answer is, "How much will a new house add to my monthly budget?"

The second question you must answer is, "Where will I get the additional funds?"

The third—and most ignored—question you must answer is, "How will I sustain the financial responsibility for this new growth?"

Let's look at each of these more closely.

"How much will a new house add to my monthly budget?"

When ascertaining additional monthly costs to buy a new house, take ALL associated expenses into account. The most obvious is the difference between your current mortgage/rent payment and the new mortgage/rent payment. Add to that things like property taxes, higher heating and cooling bills, anticipated "big ticket" maintenance items and upkeep for the next five to ten years, like roofing, siding, resurfacing the driveway or installing a new furnace.

Once this amount is determined, answer the next question.

"Where will I get the additional funds?"

For our example, let's assume that the additional increase to your housing expenses is $1,200 per month. Obviously, if your current income has only $400 per month to allot to the new house, the decision is easy: "No can do."

The decision becomes more difficult when you determine you can, in fact, eke out an extra $1,200 per month to put toward the new house. But don't start celebrating yet. Why? Because being able to pay the new house payment every month stops short of answering our third—and most important—question.

"How will I sustain the financial responsibility for this new growth?"

Before making life-changing decisions, it's important to examine the possible impact of those decisions on your future. For example, are you sacrificing other areas of your finances to support the increased monthly payment? These sacrifices might include: putting less (or nothing) into a savings account, eliminating yearly vacations, or postponing your contributions to a retirement

account. Also consider the "what if" factor of your decisions that encompasses unplanned events and emergencies. *What if:* you lose your job, experience a cut in pay, have a debilitating accident or unexpected long term health problems not covered by insurance?

If your finances are secure enough to account for sustainability, then buy that big, beautiful house and move in. But, if your increased risk outpaces your potential gain, this type of growth would do more harm than good at this stage in your life. Take a step back and implement a new plan to get you where you want to go.

So many decisions are driven by emotion, ego, and greed—to our detriment. You can change that by thinking less about what you can afford, and more about what you can sustain.

Apply the set of questions on the previous pages to each major decision in your life. Answer honestly. Growth must be controlled to be sustainable.

In 2004, a partner and I purchased a bar/restaurant in downtown Minneapolis and agreed to change the theme from a family restaurant to a modern sports bar. We had the entire place painted, had new signage installed both outside and inside, purchased flat screen TVs and redesigned the menu. At the surface it would appear that we were well on our way to success. Well, it didn't take long for that beautifully paved road to turn to gravel. Here's why:

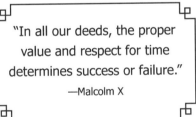

"In all our deeds, the proper value and respect for time determines success or failure."
—Malcolm X

At the time of the purchase, I lived in Las Vegas—that was problem number 1. Problems number 2, 3, 4 and 5 were that neither of us had managed a bar or restaurant, we both had full time careers, neither one of us slowed down long enough to put our plan in writing and, what's more embarrassing, neither of us can accurately account for how much money we lost. How could that possibly happen? We never established a real accounting system. This could easily go down as my biggest financial blunder ever.

Just like businesses, successful individuals control growth by developing a strategic plan.

Growth Aligned With Vision

Let's take a quick look at what we can learn from this chapter's case study company, DuPont.

DuPont's growth has always been in line with its vision. It sets financial benchmarks and remains steadfast in its principles. Corporate decision-makers keep a watchful eye on the impact that today's decisions have on future generations of the company. Responsibility begins with building value into products and services, which attracts long term and loyal customers.

> "The single biggest difference between financial success and financial failure is how well you manage your money. It's simple: to master money, you must manage money."
>
> —T. Harv Eker, Secrets of the Millionaire Mind

Sustainability is the lynchpin of DuPont's mission, which demonstrates to shareholders, employees, and partners its unwavering commitment to keep their interests at the forefront.

To achieve a level of happiness and success in your business-of-one life, you must develop these same disciplines. DuPont has been in business for more than two hundred years, and you should strive for your legacy to live on just as long.

Strategy for Growth

Simply put, strategy is a road map of the actions a business or a person takes to fulfill a mission.

The bar/restaurant purchase is also a perfect example of what can happen when there's no strategy in place for growth. Clearly I was not at a place where I could sustain that purchase, as well as all of my other financial obligations.

In business, the strategic plan determines where an organization is going over a period of time (a year, two years, five years, etc.), how it's going to get there, and how it will know if it got there or not. The strategic plan answers a range of simple questions like:

What does the business look like today?

How did we get where we are?

What do we want the business to look like (two, five, ten) years from now?

How will we get where we want to go?

When will we get there?

What will it cost?

Likewise, your life's strategic plan details the actions you will take to achieve your goals and you will be answering a similar set of questions.

Despite the simplicity of the questions, the quality of your strategic plan depends on the quality of your answers. Each question deserves your careful thought and, if necessary, additional research.

But here's the good news: a strategic plan requires a vision and mission. Since you have already created your vision and mission statements, you are well on your way to establishing a well thought-out strategic plan for your life of prosperity.

Benefits of Strategic Planning	
Business	**Prosperous Life**
Asks and answers questions of key importance to the organization	Asks and answers questions of key importance to self and family
Provides a framework for decision making throughout the organization	Provides a framework for decision making throughout your life
Reveals and clarifies future opportunities and threats	Reveals and clarifies future opportunities and threats in your life and community
Sets specific objectives for achievement	Sets specific objectives for achievement of your personal goals
Provides a basis for measuring performance	Provides a basis for measuring how closely you are adhering to your vision and mission
Serves as a channel of communication of corporate vision and mission to employees and shareholders	Serves as a channel of communication of personal vision and mission to yourself and family (stakeholders)
Develops a team focused on the organization's future	Organizes your family as a team focused on its future
Provides managerial training	Provides life skills training

As you can see, strategic planning for businesses is very similar to strategic planning for your life of prosperity; *life is a business!*

Fighting Back Life's Temptations

Ah! Sweet temptation! A little impulsive indulgence never hurt anyone, right?

Maybe not if you're talking about eating two cupcakes instead of one on your birthday, but when an indulgence starts draining your financial reserves, it's time to take a closer look at your motivation for your actions.

Whoever coined the catchphrase, "Keeping up with the Joneses" encapsulated the perfect depiction of our obsession to view our accumulation of material things as cultural superiority.

This measure of wealth or success is skewed both in business and in life. Having "stuff" is not a true indication of wealth. Many of those "Joneses" you are trying to keep up with are quietly and quickly spiraling into financial ruin. We must focus on managing our own lives instead of concerning ourselves with the lives of others. Surprisingly — especially to me — I learned this by observing a simple card game.

My brother Corey is a fierce card player. Several years ago I was with him at a card party and he was his usual confident self, winning and making sure his opponents knew he was beating them. At one point in the game, he turned to the person on his right and tipped his hand to show the guy every card he held. Later that night, I asked him why he would show his opponent his hand. Corey replied, "I didn't think he was a good enough card player to play both his hand and mine."

Corey's response stayed with me ever since. In some ways it has become a metaphor for my life. In life, we have to first master the management of our own lives before concerning ourselves with what others are doing. In other words, stop trying to keep up with the Joneses. Live in your truth!

Although I learned this lesson, I didn't learn it soon enough. I plead "guilty" to getting trapped into equating "stuff" with "status" and impulsively buying what I wanted when I wanted it, even if it meant going further into debt. My vice? I'm a watch junky. Not too many years ago I was walking through a mall, people watching and glancing at shop window displays. As I was passing a jewelry store, something particularly shiny and elegant caught my eye, and I was compelled to go inside. Twenty minutes later, I had purchased a nearly $15,000 watch using my American Express card. You read that right—$15,000.

Let me just say, the watch that I "had" to have, was one of the most irresponsible purchases I have ever made. My "need" to have it was immediate—and fleeting. Before long, I was searching for my next "fix" to showcase on my wrist.

I can guarantee you this: no, and I repeat, no, Fortune 500 Company would make a decision "on the fly" like the one I made that day. This purchase showed up nowhere in my budget (the budget that only existed in my head); it was a decision based solely on emotion. Emotionally-charged decisions are detrimental to sustainable growth. The proof? I eventually pawned that watch for a fraction of what I paid.

In 2007, I thought I had finally turned a corner. I was blessed with a financial "re-up" by selling a piece of land I co-owned in Las Vegas. The check I received at the closing was more than most Americans make in five years. I paid off all of my debt and felt I was back on my feet with a clean slate.

> "Academic qualifications are important and so is financial education. They're both important and schools are forgetting one of them."
> —Robert Kiyosaki, Rich Dad Poor Dad

Within a year, I had blown through the remainder of the money and was back to square one. Why? At that time I still hadn't "gotten it." I still had no clear vision, did not have a strategic plan for growth and sustainability, and refused to budget my finances.

I think it's time to start a new trend. Instead of showing off material things, buying more stuff to keep up with the Joneses, and trying to "out-dazzle" each other, let's start "exceeding the Joneses" by living a life of prosperity built on sustainable growth. I am all for having the finer things in life; things that are a "want

57

to have" not necessarily a "need to have." However, I have learned that these "want to haves" should not be a precursor to financial ruin. I still want "things," I just want to be able to sustain them.

Education

A good friend of mine once told me he felt he was too old to be in school. Respectfully, I told him that made no sense. Education is the only way we better ourselves and it plays a major role in managing your life to prosperity. In fact, education is essential to sustainable growth. For the past year and a half, I have been taking business classes at a community college. I've been doing this, not for the purpose of attaining a degree, but to improve skills that I knew were my weaknesses, such as accounting and advertising/marketing. This additional education helps me better manage my life.

Yet, learning doesn't happen only in day-long schoolrooms where you sit in a desk, raise your hand to speak, and bring an apple for the teacher. The Internet alone puts a wealth of education at your fingertips just waiting for you to click "Search." We are lucky to have a multitude of ways to educate ourselves. For example, you can take evening classes at the nearby community college, attend seminars, participate in webinars, read books, listen to podcasts, and vow to learn one new thing each week on the computer software you already own. *HINT: If it has anything to do with money management, strive to become a master at it!*

> "Education is the passport to the future, for tomorrow belongs to those who prepare for it today."
> —Malcolm X

Some learning opportunities will be free and some will cost you a little. But it will be money well spent if you think of it as an investment to become the CEO of your life. Start by educating yourself on things that already affect your life. For example, do you understand the charges associated with your monthly bills? How about the monetary consequences for bouncing a check?

58

What interest rates are you paying for credit cards, mortgages, and loans and how do they suck more money out of your pocket than you should have to pay? Obtaining information on these issues is crucial to your understanding of your expenses and the charges associated with your spending.

Taking the need for educating yourself a step further, what do you know about your retirement account? If you are self employed how do you save for retirement? If you are considering buying a home for the first time do you understand

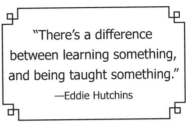

"There's a difference between learning something, and being taught something."
—Eddie Hutchins

the different types of mortgages available to you? Education is crucial even if you currently possess a post-secondary degree. The education I am talking about is not just academic; it's a "path to prosperity" education. That means being educated in the topics that will allow you to live a life of prosperity. As you continue to read through this book, take notes on the things you need to learn more about. Don't feel bad if there are concepts that you don't understand or never heard of before. This is your chance to learn—make the most of this opportunity.

The more you educate yourself, the more stable—and sustainable—your life of prosperity will be.

SWOT

Have you ever heard the acronym S-W-O-T? The letters stand for Strengths, Weaknesses, Opportunities, and Threats, and companies often perform SWOT analyses to evaluate the business or a specific project or product of the business. It is used as part of a company's strategic planning process. The Strengths and Weaknesses of the business deal with internal factors and the Opportunities and Threats deal with external factors.

By identifying areas of strengths and weaknesses a company can better plan for corporate growth by enhancing and utilizing its strengths and finding ways to improve on its weaknesses. By identifying opportunities and threats, a company can determine how it should market or change or grow its business, remaining mindful of both potential opportunities and threats.

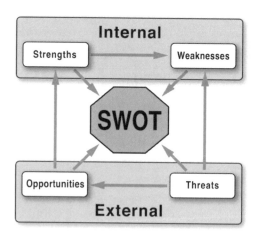

As you prepare to sharpen your skills as the CEO of your prosperous life, it's a good idea for you to perform a SWOT Analysis too. In fact, by conducting a SWOT Analysis for yourself and family members, you will pinpoint specific areas that you should focus on for education. As companies apply this analysis to their business, so must you apply it to yours; your business is YOU.

Exercise 1:   **Perform a SWOT Analysis**

A SWOT Analysis is divided into four areas. These areas are contained under two categories. Strengths and Weaknesses fall under the Internal category. Opportunities and Threats fall under the External category.

Use the matrix below to identify your SWOT characteristics. Start with Strengths and Weaknesses, followed by Opportunities and Threats.

I've included a few questions to help you get started:

Strengths
- What advantages do you have that others don't have?
- What do you do better than anyone else?
- What do other people tell you they see as your strengths?
- Which of your achievements are you most proud of?
- What values do you believe in that others fail to exhibit?

Consider this from your own perspective, and from the point of view of the people around you. Be objective and don't be modest.

TIP: If you have difficulty identifying your strengths, simply write down a list of your personal characteristics. Many of them will be strengths.

Weaknesses
- What tasks do you avoid because you don't feel confident doing them?
- What will the people around you see as your weaknesses?
- Are you completely confident in your education and skills? If not, where are you weakest?
- Do you have personality traits that hold you back?

Opportunities
- What technology can help you better manage your life?
- What educational opportunities are available to you and how can you access them?
- Do you have a network of contacts who can offer good advice?

TIP: Review your strengths. Do they open up new opportunities? Review your weaknesses. What opportunities might arise if you eliminate them?

Threats
- What obstacles do you currently face at work?
- What obstacles do you currently face at home?
- Could any of your weaknesses lead to threats?
- What obstacles have you created for yourself in the past due to poor planning/choices? (Be honest!)

Strengths	Weaknesses

Opportunities	Threats

Performing this analysis will often provide key information – it can point out what needs to be done and put problems into perspective.

Exercise 2:   **Develop a Personal Strategic Plan for Your Prosperous Life**

Although the idea of creating an action plan may sound daunting, it doesn't have to be perfect and it doesn't have to be fancy. What's important is that you block out a couple of hours and give it your undivided attention. Here's an eight-step process to get you started using one aspect of my life's vision—to obtain optimum health and wellness—as an example.

Step One – State Your Vision.

This step is easy since you created your Vision Statement in Chapter 1.

As I just stated, a piece of my vision is to obtain optimum health and wellness.

Step Two – Identify Your Mission.

Another easy step—you also created your Mission Statement in Chapter 1. My mission, in relation to my vision for optimum health and wellness, is to increase the strength of my body through engaging in exercises that build strength, endurance and personal satisfaction

Step Three – Take a Personal Inventory/SWOT.

The SWOT (Strengths, Weaknesses, Opportunities, Threats) analysis allows you to take an objective look at what you do well and what you need to work on. Lucky you! You just completed this step in Exercise 1. The SWOT analysis that I created for my physical fitness goal is:

Strengths	Weaknesses
• Mentally tough • Generally healthy • Self Motivated • Self-Employed (flexibility)	• Picky eater • Dislike of vegetables • Never eat breakfast • Still drinking alcohol
Opportunities	**Threats**
• Support of Spouse and Community • Easy gym accessibility • Access to Internet and other information resources	• Friends encouraging behavior counter to my goal achievement • Social events that include alcoholic beverages • Family & situational stressors

Step Four – Define Goals and Objectives.

Goals and objectives are like stepping stones to achieve your vision and mission. You develop them by looking at the results of your SWOT analysis and reviewing your vision and mission statements.

Write two to five objectives that give action to your mission/ vision and will take a few years to achieve. Then, develop goals to achieve each objective. Goals should be measurable, achievable, and support your objectives. Effective goals use a timeline, stating what the action is, when it is to be accomplished, and by whom. Make sure both your goals and objectives build on your strengths; shore up your weaknesses; capitalize on your opportunities; and recognize your threats.

I set several goals to reach my objective of physical health. One goal included running a marathon. Running a marathon required a strategic plan. This example is ironic in the sense that life/business is much like a marathon. You may have heard the saying that "life is not a sprint, it's a marathon." Business and life should focus on the "long haul," the future. This requires vision, mission and a strategic plan to achieve the things you seek to achieve in life. I set two objectives for myself when planning for the marathon:

Objective #1: Run a Marathon

Goal #1:   Complete the Marathon
Goal #2:   Beat Oprah Winfrey's Marathon Time –
            4 hours: 29 min.: 20 sec.
Goal #3:   Establish and Complete a Weekly
            Running Schedule

Objective #2: Raise Money for my Friend's Daughter

My friend's daughter was injured in a car accident. I used my marathon training and ran to raise money for her.

Goal #1:   To increase awareness of her injuries through
           the radio, word of mouth and the marathon itself.
Goal #2:   Raise funds for medical expenses and to support
           the family. There was no predetermined
           dollar amount set prior to beginning the process.

I completed the marathon in 4 hours and 41 minutes. Objective #1, Goal #1 was met. It was measurable in that either I would complete the race or I would drop out of the race. It was realistic considering my age, ability and training.

Goal #2 was measurable, realistic and achievable as well, even though I did not achieve this goal.

Notice that Objective #2 does not quite meet the expectations of goal setting that I defined for you in Step Four since I didn't establish a dollar amount. This is because I did not have the necessary tools to develop a strategic plan for myself at the time. I was successful in establishing a training schedule for myself that provided measurable and achievable results. However, although my second objective was for a good cause, the goals were not measurable.

Be sure to make goals that are measurable, realistic and achievable.

Step Five – Assess Your Resources.

Once you've completed your goals and objectives, it is time to assess the resources you have to accomplish them. Do your goals make financial sense? Do you have enough time to spend working to achieve your goals? If not, how can you free additional time (or money) to jump that hurdle and move forward?

Running a marathon takes a significant time commitment, so time was the biggest resource that I had to harness. I had to find the time to run and stay committed to the time by not letting anything interfere. When I looked at the time that I was awake during the day I realized the true meaning in the saying "there is just not enough time in a day." I determined that I needed more hours in my day in order to accomplish the training needed to run a marathon. Therefore, I started to get up an hour earlier to gain that additional time.

In addition to time, I needed a place to run. Living in Minnesota can create a barrier to training in that there are months throughout the year that are just too damn cold to run outside. I needed to purchase a health club membership to utilize during the winter months. This was a business decision that I needed to work into my family budget. You remember my budget, don't you? The one that was only in my head!

Whatever resources you need to realize your vision and mission must be worked into your family budget before you commit the resources to it. We will discuss this more in Key Principle #3, which is the next chapter.

Step Six – Take Action.

Review your goals and prepare a to-do list for each one by answering this question, "What roadblocks exist to achieving my goal?" Use the answer to write your action items. Then, assign deadlines for completion to stay on task.

My to-do list for running the marathon basically consisted of the following:

- Change my diet – determine what I was eating, what I should be eating and what I needed to supplement
- Determine the type of clothing and running shoes needed
- Find a health club
- Research marathon training schedules
- Create my training schedule
- Calculate distances for running locations (i.e., lakes, parks, trails)
- Learn stretching exercises and how to avoid injury
- Develop a list of "affirmations" to encourage myself as the training progressed

Step Seven – Keep Track.

In step four, you wrote goals that were measurable. Put these targets on a spreadsheet and keep track of your progress. Determine "how" you want to track your progress. You can track your progress on a continuum (scale) to make sure you are on target and making progress. Or you can track your progress by having a checklist to check off the completed items as you go along. I suggest that you do both. Different goals work better under a scale than a checklist. For example, goals that have a specific time line or amount you may want to use a continuum.

Preparation for Running a Full Marathon
Check List Method

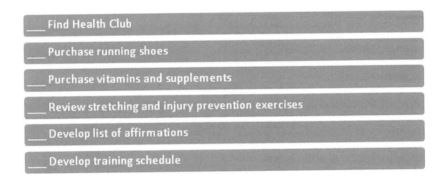

GOAL: RUN A FULL MARATHON
Measuring Training Progress on a Continuum

Step Eight – Make a Habit of Strategizing.

To emulate great business leaders, keep raising the bar. As goals are achieved, set new ones. Pay attention to needed adjustments

or adapting when the environment changes. If you have a family, communicate your goals and expectations for participation by each member. Make strategic planning a life-long habit.

Remember:

- The real benefit of the strategic planning process is the process, not the document.
- There is no "perfect" plan. Do your best strategizing, learn from what you're doing, and do better the next time around.
- The strategic planning process is a series of small moves that together keep you headed in the right direction.

Start simple, start small—but start!

My strategy for completing the marathon was to not only train for the marathon but to make permanent life changes while training for the marathon. Developing affirmations is also a strategy. These affirmations allowed me to motivate myself when I needed that extra push. Lastly, I focused on my future instead of my past. I imaged a different life for myself. I did not know it then but the life that I imagined was a life of prosperity that emulates a business.

Your life of prosperity requires more from you than deciding what you want your life to look like. It requires a strong, stable foundation to steady everything you pile on top of it. Laying the foundation for your future starts by understanding and embracing the concept of controlled growth. You control growth by developing and implementing a strategic plan. Your strategic plan, in one word, is ACTION!

Paramount to the successful execution of your plan is ongoing education. When I speak about education, I don't necessarily mean formal education that earns accredited degrees that you can display on your wall. It's about learning a little something of value in life every day. These baby steps give your business a better chance of success over time. Using a SWOT analysis, you will pinpoint what you do well and what you should learn to do better. Life is a learning process and you never stop learning. However, active learning is required to achieve a life of prosperity. You must actively seek out the information that you need to be successful.

By incorporating these discoveries into your strategic plan, you'll be well on your way to having the life of prosperity you deserve. Now that you have foundation and a strategic plan to carry out your life's vision and mission, the following Key Principles help to enhance the quality of your prosperous life. Keep moving forward.

☙ Key Principle #2 ❧

Sustainable Growth & Education

Keep strong, steady growth and a commitment to
education at the forefront of your vision.

*Accelerated growth without a strong foundation and
sustainable long-term plan leads to chaos and erosion.*

Chapter 3

Key Principle #3

Financial Literacy & Stability

Financial Literacy & Stability

=

Fiscal Responsibility

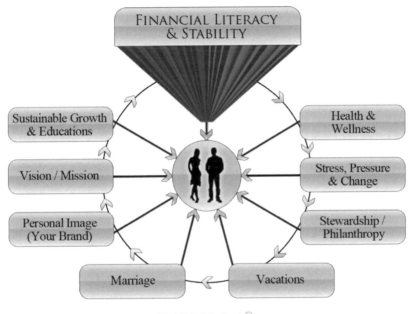

The Life Is A Business! ™
Blueprint To Prosperity

"The number one problem in today's generation and economy is the lack of financial literacy."

— Alan Greenspan

Best Buy

Best Buy CEO:	Brian J. Dunn
Number of Employees:	180,000
Fortune 500 Ranking:	#45
Industry:	Consumer Electronics
Location:	Richfield, MN
Annual Revenue:	$49.0B

The biggest consumer electronics outlet in the U.S. is also the best — Best Buy, that is. The company operates more than 1,400 stores throughout the U.S. and Canada, and another 2,600 stores in Europe, mostly under the Best Buy, Best Buy Mobile, and The Car Phone Warehouse banners. The stores sell a wide variety of electronic gadgets, movies, music, computers, and appliances.

In addition to selling products, Best Buy offers installation and maintenance services, technical support, and subscriptions for cell phone and Internet services. As the dominant consumer electronics chain in the U.S., following the demise of rival Circuit City, Best Buy is looking abroad for growth.[1]

---

1 www.hoovers.com

❧ Follow the Money ❧

When business owners want to know how well their companies are doing, they need only to heed one simple rule: Follow the Money. They take a good long look at what's coming in and what's going out. If the incoming money exceeds all of the expenses, then it's been a good year. If they are spending more than they are bringing in and going into debt to keep up with expenses, then it's been a bad year. Too many bad years, and they'll be out of business.

If you want to know exactly where you are in your life, heed the same rule: Follow the Money. Know where your money is coming from, how much it is, and where it is going. It's pretty simple stuff. Yet, so many of us shy away from keeping track of our money. We tend to "guesstimate" what we earn and what we spend, living in the moment rather than planning for a lifetime. Your life of prosperity requires more from you. And, although you may begrudgingly adopt a 'fiscally responsible' habit, once it becomes part of your routine and you experience the difference it makes, you'll be sending me a "thank you" card.

I know, I know… you don't have a head for numbers and mathematics wasn't your best subject in school. It doesn't matter—I'm not going to ask you to do calculus or find the square root of anything. I'm confident you have the basic skills required to learn how to keep a simple budget.

Benefits and Perks of Creating a Budget

Before I get to the benefits of having a budget, I want to clear up one huge misconception. People think that budgets restrict spending. The truth is that a budget can expand your spending—you get more of what you want because you've taken the time to figure out how to get it—without going into debt. Another misconception is that budgets are static. Not true. Budgets are fluid. You change them to fit your priorities. The simple goal is to work with the money you have to get the things you want (including some "fun" money) and plan for expected and unexpected expenses. You've worked hard for your money and it's time for your money to work hard for you. Your money will only work hard for you if you are in control. The way to take control is by creating a budget.

Benefits of creating a budget include:
- **Stress Reducer.** One of the biggest contributors to stress is money problems. When you have too much debt and can't pay the bills, the stress level goes up. In fact, statistics show that arguments over money are a leading cause of divorce. Having and keeping to a budget significantly reduces stress, gets family members involved in financial goals, and eliminates the "blame game" of who overspends each month.
- **Helps Uncover "Extra" Money.** The simple act of tracking your income and expenses puts you in control. Accounting for every penny that comes in and goes out will expose frivolous spending — like buying a cup of coffee and doughnut you didn't really want at the convenience store when you stopped to fill up the gas tank, or buying a second pair of shoes because they were on sale, not because you need — or even want — them.
- **Saves Time.** Whether you do your own taxes or send them to someone else each year, how much time do you spend collecting information at the end of the year? With a budget, all of your expenses and income are documented, including taxes.
- **Lets You Plan for the Future.** When will you be able to buy a new car? Your budget will tell you. How much can you spend for a vacation? Your budget will tell you. How about saving for retirement, college funds, and emergencies? Your budget will help you allocate funds to reach all of those goals.
- **Feels Good.** If you're reducing stress, finding extra money, saving time, and planning for your future, how can you NOT

74

feel good about it? The rewards are not only monetary, but build your self-esteem and self-confidence. When you're in charge of your finances, you're finally in charge of your life.

Characteristics of a Well-Managed Business and Life

So if the rule for financial health is to "follow the money," how do you go about doing it? You do what the "big guys" do but on a much smaller scale.

According to a Dunn & Bradstreet report, a well-managed business, at a minimum, has the following characteristics:

- It is more liquid than a badly managed company (has money in the bank)
- The balance sheet is as important to the owner as the income statement
- Stability is emphasized, instead of rapid growth
- Long range planning is important

Your well-managed life should have these exact same characteristics.

Characteristics of a Well-Managed Business / Life	
Business	**Prosperous Life**
More liquid than badly managed company (has money in the bank)	Has money in the bank, i.e. savings, retirement fund, etc.
Owner views Balance Sheet as important as Income Statement	Pays attention to what you owe as well as what you earn
Emphasizes stability rather than growth	Focuses on maintaining stability
Prioritizes long range planning	Plans for the future

Finances are Key to a Stable Life

Finance and accounting tend to sound more complicated because we throw around terms like, "financial statement,"

"balance sheet," and "cash flow." Then we add a few more phrases, like "fiscal responsibility," "assets and liabilities," and "liquidity." I'll admit that, in a big corporation, finances can become more complicated as it grows and expands by taking on subsidiaries, or running independent divisions. The bigger the company, the more complicated its finance and accounting system.

But for your business life—and your financial health—99 times out of 100, you'll be just fine if you keep your focus on what's coming in and where it's going. When you do, you'll start scrutinizing what you've done with your money, what you're doing with it today, and projecting what to do with it long term.

It's no accident that Best Buy, this chapter's case study, is the last man standing in its battle with competitors. The company excels at careful and well thought-out financial decision-making, which takes skill, literacy and discipline. Best Buy makes major purchasing decisions only after months—in some cases, years—of planning. Best Buy, like any great corporation, distinguishes between 'wants' and 'needs'—and so should you. Basically, you only need four things to survive:

- Shelter
- Enough food and water to maintain your health
- Basic health care and hygiene products
- Clothing to remain appropriately dressed for business and relaxation

Anything beyond these four basics—a big house, name-brand clothing, going to fancy restaurants, a new car—is a want. Wants are okay but only after your needs are met.

Does this mean you can only buy things you need? Of course not. Life is meant to be lived, not merely survived. But it is important to recognize the difference between wants and needs as you build your financial well being and strike a balance for stability.

I learned the hard way what the consequences are for not having a budget or plan for sustained growth. In 2005, I lived in a 4,400 square foot home, in a Las Vegas guard-gated community. I regularly hosted out-of-town visitors, went to prize fights, owned a sports bar in downtown Minneapolis, Minnesota, had "his and hers" foreign sedans, enjoyed an awesome watch collection, ate at the finest five-star steak houses, and traveled on a whim. By 2006, it was gone.

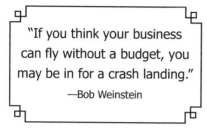

"If you think your business can fly without a budget, you may be in for a crash landing."

—Bob Weinstein

I could not sustain my lifestyle because I had no bookkeeping system, no real budget set up and no plan to track my income, expenses and plan for growth. I didn't have a clue how well my portfolio was — or wasn't — performing. I was flying by the seat of my pants and I suddenly found myself careening toward the ground without a parachute. *Lights out, party over!*

My brick-and-mortar house was beautiful and my "financial house" was a mess. When the lack of budgeting, tracking, and planning became evident, it was too late to fix. I've slowly rebuilt my life — the right way — using the principles tied to having a life of prosperity.

When you follow the money, you make better decisions, and getting your "financial house" in order is the key to a stable life.

Learn to Read the Fine Print

In 2004, I was reviewing the utility bill for one of the properties I owned. I must admit that I did not usually "review" bills, I just wrote the checks to pay them. For some reason, this particular bill just seemed high so I began to "audit" the bill. I discovered that I was being charged for four garbage cans when I only had two. This cost me an additional $60 per month. I had been paying this erroneous bill for well over six months and never noticed it. Keep in mind that I had over 50 units at the time yet, upon discovering this error, I never took the time to check the other bills to see if I was being overcharged for them, too. When I think back to that incident I now recognize the symbolism; I was literally throwing money away.

We only need to look at our country's own economic state to see how we've become a nation of financially illiterate individuals who pursued what they wanted more than securing what they needed. We're seeing a record number of foreclosures, bankruptcies, repossessions, and credit card companies getting rich off of late fee charges. Utility companies, banks and cellular phone companies make billions of "extra" dollars every year because of our financial irresponsibility. Many businesses count on you and me to make impulse buying decisions and enter into emotionally-driven contracts without reading the fine print. While banks are notorious for this, there is plenty of "fine print" to go around with added fees, "mystery" charges, and can't-get-out-of-it clauses you failed to notice.

Ally Bank has been running a series of commercials that succinctly make this point. I urge you to visit YouTube.com to search for some of them, all primarily using children in the ads. In one particular commercial (http://www.youtube.com/watch?v=QgdTymCZowU), a young boy is gathering colorful eggs and putting them into a basket that sits atop a table. A man in a suit is seated at the table, reading a newspaper. As the boy turns away to retrieve more eggs, the man says, "You're doing a great job," while at the same time, taking most of the eggs out of the basket.

When the boy returns, he notices the basket is now practically empty and says to the man, "Why did you take my eggs?" The man answers, "Egg management fee." The boy asks, "What's an egg management fee?" The man simply repeats emphatically, "Egg management fee!" One of the many messages in this commercial is that there are vague and nonsensical answers to the boy's question. The man was simply stealing the boy's eggs. Because of our irresponsible nature, these companies don't have to work very hard to steal ours.

Who is stealing YOUR eggs? Take a closer look at some of your bills to see what kind of "mystery" fees you pay. Do you pay your bills late each month? Then you are likely paying a late fee the following month. Are you skipping a credit card payment every once in awhile or exceeding the limit? Then your interest rates on purchases have most likely been bumped up a notch. In fact, default interest rates—the penalty rates charged when you violate the terms of your card agreement—can be two or three times higher than the initial credit card rate. In a 2009 study conducted by Applied Research and Consulting LLC, results showed 36 percent of respondents didn't know the interest rate on the credit card they used most often.

It is time to identify the companies that are stealing from your basket of eggs, uncover how they're doing it, and determine how you can stop it. It all begins by taking control of your finances.

The Basics of Your Financial Health

Essential to every business is the creation of a solid financial plan. Fortune 500 companies all use the same method of financial planning consisting of three primary documents: a Balance Sheet, Income Statement, and Cash Flow Statement.

The **balance sheet** summarizes a company's 1) assets, 2) liabilities, and 3) shareholders' equity. These three components give the owner — or demonstrate to potential investors — an account of what the company owns and owes, as well as the amount invested by shareholders.

The balance sheet follows the formula:
Assets = Liabilities + Shareholders' Equity

Your *personal* **balance sheet** lists current assets and long-term assets, and current and long-term liabilities. Current assets include cash in your checking and savings account (and the secret stash under your mattress!). Long-term assets include common stock and real estate, shown at market value. Current liabilities include loan debt and mortgage debt due. Long-term liabilities include mortgage and other loans. Your personal net worth is the difference between your total assets and total liabilities.

Your **net worth** is a very important number in determining your financial health and setting realistic financial goals. An example of a personal balance sheet is shown below. As I discussed earlier, had I paid closer attention to my financial picture, I would have come to the conclusion that I did not need to own 50 housing units to achieve the financial "goals" I had for my life. Although my net worth was positive, I used it as a trophy. I never used it as a "tool" in my strategic plan to achieve my goals. I never established goals to maintain that net worth in the future or determine if I had the income, or would continue to have the income, to sustain the effects of future liabilities.

Sample Balance Sheet

Robert & Jane Doe
Fortune 500 Ave N.
Balance Sheet
As of December 31, 2010

Assets

Cash On Hand	$100.00
Cash at Bank	$4,000.00
Stocks and Bonds	$2,500.00
401K	$8,000.00
Personal Real Estate	$200,000.00
Investment Real Estate	$90,000.00
Personal Property	$3,600.00
Auto	$6,000.00
Other Assets	$3,000.00
Total Assets	$317,200.00

Liabilities

Auto Loan	$10,000.00
Credit Cards	$15,000.00
Home Mortgage	$160,000.00
Investment Real Estate	$70,000.00
Student Loans	$25,000.00
Total Liabilities	$280,000.00
Net Worth	**$37,200.00**

An **income statement** measures a company's financial performance over a specific accounting period. Financial performance is assessed by giving a summary of how the business incurs its revenues and expenses through both operating and non-operating

81

activities. It also shows the net profit or loss incurred over a specific accounting period, typically over a fiscal quarter or year. The income statement is also referred to as a financial statement, profit and loss statement (P&L), or statement of revenue and expense.

A *personal* income statement is like a financial motion picture of your cash inflows and outflows. It can be an effective budgeting tool since it helps you analyze expenses and revenues over a period of time.

A **cash flow statement** provides collective data about cash inflows a company receives from ongoing operations and external investment sources. It also shows all cash outflows for business activities and investments. A cash flow statement is one of several quarterly financial reports any publicly traded company is required to disclose to the SEC and the public.

Your *personal* **cash flow** is simply the mathematical difference between your cash inflows and cash outflows.

At first glance, all of this financial jargon might seem intimidating, but I assure you that you do not need to be an accounting major to create a solid financial plan for your life. The basic document you need to develop is a budget.

The Foundation of a Sound Budget

Financial literacy and stability begin with a sound budget. A budget is a plan that outlines your financial goals. So a budget may be thought of as an action plan. Planning a budget helps you allocate resources (paycheck/income), evaluate your performance (how well you are managing your paycheck/income), and allows you to formulate current and future financial goals for you and your family. A budget is basically a snapshot of your current financial picture.

While planning a budget can occur at any time,

> "We were not taught financial literacy in school. It takes a lot of work and time to change your thinking and to become financially literate."
> —Robert Kiyosaki, Rich Dad Poor Dad

82

for many businesses, planning a budget is an annual task, where the past year's budget is reviewed and budget projections are made for the next three or even five years. This should be the same for your personal financial situation. A budget should be drafted and reviewed and revised as needed on a monthly basis, at least in the beginning.

Budgeting begins by knowing two things:
1. How much money you make (income)
2. Your total liabilities (what you spend — debt)

When you subtract your liabilities from your income, you determine your Net Worth.

What goes into a budget?

Here is an outline of budgetary considerations. Please note that estimated percentages will vary by your geographical location.

Income: Allocate 90-98% of income for your budget.
              The remaining 2-10% is for savings.
Income sources include:
- employment income
- alimony received
- investment income
- social security
- support payments
- savings

Housing Expenses: Allocate 32-35% of income if you own;
              15-20% if you rent
Housing expenses include:
- your mortgage payment with escrow (taxes, insurance)
- monthly rental payment if you do not own
- utility services (electric, gas, oil, water, sewage, garbage, etc.)
- telephone, internet, cable
- house repairs and maintenance

Transportation: Allocate 9-12% of income
Transportation expenses include:
- auto loan payments
- auto insurance
- fuel expenses
- maintenance and repairs
- taxes, licensing
- parking
- public transportation

Family or Personal Care: Allocate 8-19% of income;
                        15-25% for full child or elder care services
Family care expenses include:
- family care insurance (health, disability, life, dental, other care)
- doctor, dental, eye care, hospital visits
- veterinarian expenses
- prescriptions and over-the-counter medications
- child care
- elder care
- health clubs

Living Expenses: Allocate 27-35% of income
Home living expenses include:
- food
- home living supplies
- school and work lunches
- snacks, vendors
- clothing
- education-related expenses
- home services (cleaning, gardening)
- postage and paper supplies

Family Recreation: Allocate 4-6% of income

Recreation expenses include:

- dining out
- movies out and rentals
- outside entertainment
- cigarettes, beer, wine, liquor
- birthdays and holidays
- vacation travel
- weekend, day trips
- gambling, lottery tickets

Obligations: Allocate 18-28% of income

Obligation expenses include:

- credit card payments
- student loan payments
- home equity line or loan payments
- personal loan payments
- alimony, child support payments
- judgment or liens
- other assessed taxes
- charitable donations

NOTE: Your goal is to reduce obligation expenses.

Savings: Allocate 2-10% of income

Savings include:

- 401K contributions
- IRA contributions
- investments
- savings (personal, college, retirement)

NOTE: Your goal is to increase savings.

Budgeting, I'll admit, will take some time to set up. But every Fortune 500 Company has one and so should your life business.

Helpful Budgetary Tips

As you look at the above list of what goes into a budget, keep the following in mind:

Plan for Major Purchases

A financially damaging trend in western culture during the past decade is Impulse Buying. We wake up, decide we want a new car, go to the dealer to pick one out and finance it (notice I didn't say we buy it). Making decisions this way is fundamentally unsound and is unsustainable. Planning for major purchases is a must, and should be in accordance with your overall household budget. There's nothing wrong with pursuing the car or house of your dreams, just make sure it is strategically planned so it can be sustained.

Max Out Savings and Retirement Funds

"Pay yourself first." We've all heard this phrase and, unfortunately, most of us ignore it. Believe it or not, this is sound advice and you must follow it. Saving money is not only for the wealthy. It is, in fact, one way to become wealthy.

People and families with even the most modest incomes have the ability to save. Nearly every Fortune 500 Company offers savings and retirement plans to their employees, often matching employee contributions. If this is practiced at your place of employment, take full advantage of it.

Saving for a rainy day can actually be easy. Little exercises, like saving all your change or putting away a dollar a day, are all it takes to help develop the habit of saving.

According to the Employee Benefit Research Institute's annual Retirement Confidence Survey, the percentage of American workers who have less than $10,000 saved for retirement has grown to 43%. The number of American workers who say that they have less than $1,000 saved for retirement has grown to 27%. Don't let this be you.

Considering that both Social Security and Medicare are on the verge of collapse, you should also be aggressive with your saving strategies.

Rein In Spending Habits

Politicians have told us that, for America's economy to recover, we need to spend money. In some cases they've urged us to spend money we don't have. Ask yourself, "What sense does that make?" The answer is: NONE.

Disciplined spending habits are a must if our life business will ever give us the enjoyment life has to offer. Spending money "just to spend money" is a mindset that is crippling families and individuals who simply cannot afford it. When you understand the difference between "wants" and "needs" you can bring your spending habits under control.

Protect Yourself and Your Family with Insurance (Health and Life)

As part of your emergency preparedness plan you should always carry the correct type and amount of insurance.

Insurance, both life and health, is an important component of any sound financial plan. Insurance helps protect you and your loved ones in different ways against the cost of accidents, illness, disability, and death. There was a time when health insurance was part of a benefits plan where you worked, but with today's struggling economy, those benefits are harder to find. Insurance coverage to protect yourself and your loved ones has become your responsibility. High medical bills continue to be one of this nation's top five reasons people file for bankruptcy.

Life insurance is another key component to living and managing a life of prosperity. When people forego investing in life insurance, or have too little, family members are left to deal with the consequences, making an already difficult time more difficult.

Prepare for Catastrophe (Crisis Management)

We can't predict catastrophic events but, when they happen, there is a long and challenging recovery. As of this writing, some of the most recent devastating national events include: 9/11, Katrina, and the BP oil spill. But there are also personal catastrophes that affect our lives and finances. For example, a car accident that totals

your car, a family member who needs extensive medical care, a bad storm that floods your basement, the loss of a job, or a family-altering divorce.

These unforeseen events can be managed if you are prepared. It is imperative that you have contingency plans in place — an alternate way to get to work or getting the kids to school, adequate health insurance, and good old, reliable cash reserves.

Sample Monthy Budget

Robert & Jane Doe
Fortune 500 Ave N.
Monthly Budget

Income
Wages (after taxes)	$4,000.00
Rental Income (net)	$1,000.00
Total Income	$5,000.00

Expenses
Food	$350.00
Utilities	$385.00
Transportation (Fuel/Parking)	$190.00
Household Maint. & Repairs	$120.00
Telephone/Cable/Internet	$125.00
Insurance (auto)	$120.00
Auto Expenses (Repairs & Maint.)	$55.00
Medical Insurance & Co-Pays	$255.00
Health Club Membership	$40.00
Church Donations	$200.00
Clothing	$60.00
Savings & Investments	$150.00
401K	$100.00
Auto Loan	$250.00
Credit Cards	$400.00
Home Mortgage (Taxes/Insurance)	$925.00
Investment Real Estate	$550.00
Education Related Expenses (Student Loan)	$150.00
Family Recreation	$175.00
Other	$150.00
Total Expenses	$4,750.00

Total Income Less Expenses	**$250.00**

ᐸ Key Principle #3 ᐳ

Financial Literacy & Stability

Commit to an ongoing quest to obtain and
understand the truth about your finances so you can
stabilize your financial health and become a better
advocate for you and your family.

If you feel everyone is out to get your money, you are probably right.

Key Principle #4

Health & Wellness

Health & Wellness (Lifestyle Habits)

=

Corporate Wellness

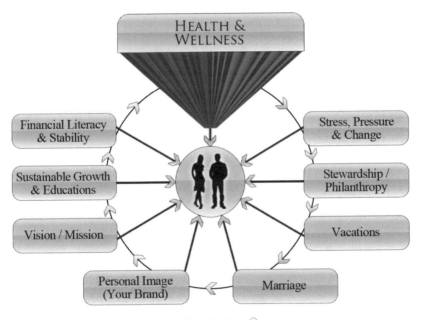

The Life Is A Business! ™
Blueprint To Prosperity

*"Just because you're not sick doesn't
mean you're healthy."*

— Author Unknown

Case Study

General Mills

General Mills CEO:	Kendall J. Powell
Number of Employees:	30,000
Fortune 500 Ranking:	#193
Industry:	Food Service
Location:	Minneapolis, MN
Annual Revenue:	$13.7B

General Mills gets its Kix trying to grab the spotlight as the U.S.' #1 breakfast cereal maker (wrangling for the top spot every year with uber-rival Kellogg). But #1 or not, the company has supermarket aisles full of kid-friendly products. Its Big G Cereals include the well-known brands Cheerios, Chex, and Wheaties. Its products are manufactured in 15 countries and available in more than 100. General Mills operates 70 production facilities — 44 in the U.S., 11 in the Asia Pacific region, three in Canada, seven in Europe, four in Latin America and Mexico, and one in South Africa.[1]

---

1 www.hoovers.com

Health Begets Wealth

Now that we've taken a close look at the importance of financial health, let's take a look at individual health. Believe it or not, a person's health dramatically impacts productivity and large corporations like General Mills understand this and capitalize on it.

Corporate wellness is one of the most important investments that a company can make in its employees. Companies that implement corporate wellness programs are not only investing in the physical wellness, safety, and mental health of their employees, but are also taking preventative measures by creating a healthier business environment. By implementing a corporate wellness program, companies are able to improve the overall productivity and are able to save money on health expenses.

Often, companies are concerned about the actual wellness ROI (return on investment) but the truth is that, by encouraging healthier lifestyles, companies are creating healthier employees who will work more diligently and miss fewer days of work due to illness.[1] Employers who invest in worksite health promotion experienced a 28% reduction in sick leave absenteeism, 26% reduction in use of health care benefits and a 30% reduction in worker's compensation claims and disability management.[2] Now, that's measurable success that equates health with wealth.

Bottom-line Benefits of Corporate Wellness Programs

Our case study company, General Mills, recognizes the bottom-line benefits of having a healthy workforce and places a high value on corporate wellness. At its corporate headquarters, employees have convenient access to services that enhance both health and quality of life, such as an on-site fitness center, healthy cooking

1 www.MyHealthCoach.com
2 American Journal of Health Promotion, 2003

classes and same-day medical appointments at the company's onsite preventive health clinic.

General Mills also gets involved outside of its corporate compound. In 2009, two of the contestants participating in the seventh season of NBC's popular reality television show, "The Biggest Loser," were from Richfield, Minnesota, a neighboring suburb to Minneapolis-based General Mills. The company decided to tie in a charity promotion, the "Pound for Pound Challenge," donating 10 cents to "Feeding America" for every pound of weight loss pledged at www.biggestloser.com.

"This is our first integrated partnership of this kind," says John Haugen, General Mills' vice president of health and wellness. "We're looking for a positive impact on all of our brands." General Mills is putting its money where its mouth is, but based on Haugen's statement, it's clear that General Mills views health and wellness as important for its bottom line as well. Aside from the obvious benefit of having happy, healthy employees, companies can save millions of dollars each year in healthcare costs and improve the productivity of their workforce by implementing a wellness program. They also induce an image boost that reflects favorably on their reputations. Bottom-line benefits for corporations include:

Increased Productivity

Research shows that employees who believe their employer has a vested interest in their well being feel better about their jobs. When they feel better about their jobs, they respond by doing a better job.

In addition to the ability to work for longer periods of time and effectively concentrate on the work, Partnerships for a Healthy Workforce (PHW) reports that a healthy workforce leads to reduced absenteeism and lost time, and can also reduce employee turnover. According to PHW, employees are "more likely to be attracted to, remain with, and value a company that obviously values them." Higher productivity, lower absenteeism, and reduced turnover all positively impact the bottom line.

Reduced Healthcare Costs

Because of the potentially large upfront investment for a wellness program, it is often difficult for companies to envision the reality of lower healthcare costs. Yet, studies repeatedly have proven that having healthy employees can dramatically decrease healthcare costs. Here are a few examples from PHW:

- "Smokers generated 31% higher claim costs than non-smokers"
- "Workers with unhealthy weights had 143% higher hospital inpatient utilization than those with healthy weights"
- Employees with just a few risk factors cost much less than employees with numerous risk factors

Savings can be realized through any scale of program – from single activities to comprehensive company-wide wellness programs. Need proof? News Press reported results of a Dallas-based company with 6,500 employees that instituted a wellness program. In just one year, and with only half of its employees participating, the company saved $500,000 in health care costs.

Enhanced Company Image

Whether it should be a factor or not, there is no disputing that a company's image is significantly enhanced when it supports the wellness of its employees. It demonstrates that the organization has a degree of social responsibility, which reflects well on the company and builds a reputation of caring and concern for its "family" of employees.

How Your Health and Wellness Affects Your Prosperous Life

Corporations may have ulterior motives to help keep employees healthy, but they know a good business decision when they see one—and so should you. Your life of prosperity includes similar "ulterior motives" for choosing to live a healthy life. Lower healthcare costs are certainly a great motivator, but consider these additional "perks" for a healthier you:

Individual Benefits of Improved Health	
Fortune 500 Corporate Employees	Your Prosperous Life
Increased concentration	Increased concentration
Increased clarity for problem-solving	Increased clarity for problem-solving
Increased energy	Increased energy
Reduced weight, lowered blood pressure and normal cholesterol levels result in reduced risk factors of diabetes and heart problems	Reduced weight, lowered blood pressure and normal cholesterol levels result in reduced risk factors of diabetes and heart problems

Hmmm. Looks like the rewards of improved employee health for corporations are exactly the same for your prosperous life. Think about it. Maintaining your physical health improves your quality of life, promotes longevity, decreases your health care expenses (long term and short term) and reduces losses from being out of work. Healthy people are typically happier, more self-confident, and motivated. What better way to live your life?

Okay, I hear you — it's easier said than done. Believe me when I tell you that I had my own struggles choosing "health" over "happenstance." While in the throes of building my flawed business empire, I was too busy to spend time in a gym and never thought twice about what I was eating. I thought I was living the good life. But, when my business (and life) started to crumble, I was overwhelmed with stress. A friend recommended that I start working out. I thought, "why not?" so in 2006 I joined a health club. Although it was more on a whim than part of a plan, it turned out to be one of the best decisions I made that year.

I met new people from all walks of life while getting myself mentally, physically and spiritually "in shape." In doing so, I noticed that I felt better, and I was smiling more. Working out took my mind off the bad things that were happening and allowed me to reflect, thinking of how I could piece my life back together.

I mentioned in a previous chapter that I trained for and ran a marathon. In fact, I ran two: one in 2006 and again in 2009, completing them both. The discipline and commitment to achieve those accomplishments spilled into the rest of my life, which is why Health and Wellness became a key principle for living a prosperous life — it is a critical, and often overlooked, business decision.

97

I continue working out, taking multi-vitamins and making improvements to my diet. Do I do everything right all of the time? No. I still have my small vices. The point is to keep striving to do better — step by step, little by little.

I want my golden years to truly be golden — and I want yours to be golden, too.

Benefits of Adopting Healthy Habits

So far, I've generalized about the benefits of living a healthy lifestyle. If you are not yet convinced that there are life-altering benefits associated with healthy habits, then let me get more specific.

Benefits of Adopting Healthy Habits	
Healthy Habit	**Benefit**
Regular exercise	• Keeps you fit • Relieves stress and tension • Fights fatigue • Burns fat and helps you lose weight • Prevents clogged arteries
Healthy eating	• Reduces risks of heart attacks, stroke and other cardiovascular disease • Provides energy • Improves your physical, mental and emotional well being • Helps you save on your health care costs
Stop smoking	Lowers your risk of getting emphysema, lung cancer and other lung-related health problems
Proper hygiene	Cleanliness of your surroundings and adopting good hygiene practices prevent external elements – bacteria, viruses, etc. – from contributing to health problems.
Rest and relaxation	A balanced, healthy lifestyle includes healthy relationships. Rest and relaxation help reduce stress. Setting aside time to do things with your spouse and/or children will improve your relationships.

Consequences of Ignoring Health Habits

The cost of not being healthy cannot truly be measured, but with millions of Americans without health care insurance, Medicare on the brink of collapse and seniors taking bus trips to Canada to have their prescriptions filled, I think it's safe to say, it's more advantageous to be healthy than to not be healthy.

Diabetes is becoming one of the world's most prevalent diseases, and its financial cost is reaching staggering proportions, too, to well over $200 billion a year in the U.S. alone.[3] Obesity is also a rapidly rising burden on the U.S. healthcare system. Obesity in the United States now carries the hefty price tag of $147 billion per year in direct medical costs, just over 9 percent of all medical spending, experts report.[4] In fact, people who are obese spend almost $1,500 more each year on health care. "A normal-weight individual will spend about $3,400 per year in medical expenditures and that number rises to about $4,870 if that individual is obese."[5] Where there is obesity, diabetes is sure to follow.

"Every day do something that will inch you closer to a better tomorrow."

—Doug Firebaugh

Add to those figures hospital co-pays, transportation expenses, cost of prescriptions and time needed to recover. These all negatively impact your bottom line; and as we get older our deteriorating health will cost us even more.

In addition to healthcare costs that are directly related to disease and physical ailments, there are also "hidden" factors that contribute to your unhealthy lifestyle. Your health and wellness involve more than getting exercise and eating right. Two of those "hidden" culprits affecting your future health are:

1. Chronic anger, stress or worry
2. Feeling out of control at home or in your relationships[6]

Surprised? Our emotions and mental health have a significant impact on our physical health and we need to pay attention to the mind/body connection of our overall health and wellness.

3 http://www.usatoday.com/news/health/2008-11-18-diabetes-cost_N.htm?POE=click-refer
4 http://abcnews.go.com/Health/Healthday/story?id=8184975&page=1
5 http://abcnews.go.com/Health/Healthday/story?id=8184975
6 Excerpt from the article, "The Deadliest Health Sins," Readers Digest online, http://www.rd.com/living-healthy/the-deadliest-health-sins/article186098.html

Mental Health: The Mind/Body Connection

CEOs know that when they are physically active they're also mentally focused and that fitness is about more than improving your physical well being; it has an effect on your mind and spirit, too. CEOs know this about themselves, and they know it about their employees. You need to know it for your life of prosperity.

Our most recent economic downturn brought with it thoughts and feelings that many Americans never before experienced. In an American Psychological Association poll in September of 2008, 80 percent of the respondents reported the economy as causing significant stress, up from 66 percent from April 2007. The National Sleep Foundation said 27 percent of people surveyed in the fall of 2007 had sleeplessness because of economic anxiety.

Serious mental illnesses (SMIs), which afflict about 6% of American adults, cost society $193.2 billion in lost earnings per year, according to findings published in the *American Journal of Psychiatry*. People suffering with SMIs reportedly earn less than people without. These types of stresses, if not dissipated, will cause any number of problems that all negatively impact one's bottom line.

How Emotions Affect Your Health

Statistics aside, you can likely pinpoint events in your life where your emotions affected your health. Perhaps you were stressed, anxious or upset and you suddenly had a headache, couldn't sleep, or felt lightheaded. Worse yet, you might have developed high blood pressure or an ulcer.

This mind/body connection is no coincidence. When you think of your body as a "human machine" you can better understand that, when one part is not working correctly, it affects the performance of the entire machine.

Poor emotional health can also weaken your body's immune system, making you more likely to get colds and other infections during emotionally difficult times. And, when you are feeling stressed, anxious or upset, you may not take care of your health as well as you should.

Sleep Deprivation and the Importance of Rest

In our culture, we are often led to believe that anything can be achieved by hard work, and hard work only. But we all know we can't keep performing at our peak level without occasional breaks. For a while, we may be able to cheat, push through, and force ourselves to stay focused to get the job done. However, eventually we reach the point where we are just too exhausted, drained, bored or uninspired to go any further. We will be unable to muster enough energy to get another project started. We may stare at problems, puzzled, confused and unable to solve them. We may begin to procrastinate for no obvious reasons. We may not be able to see the proverbial forest for the trees. In this state of mind, the smartest thing to do is to press the pause button....and rest.

Early in my entrepreneurial career, late 1999, I worked at least 16 hours per day. These were just the hours that I was physically at the office and do not include other time spent working and/or thinking about work outside of the office. Not only was my body rarely at rest, my mind was never at rest. This was a bad habit that I carried with me through my good times and throughout my "fall." I never recognized the importance of both rest and sleep and how critical both were to the growth of my business. I know now that this actually contributed to the eventual failure of my business.

> "Money is a result, wealth is a result, health is a result, illness is a result, your weight is a result. We live in a world of cause and effect."
>
> —T. Harv Eker, Secrets of the Millionaire Mind

Getting adequate rest and sleep are key to living a life of prosperity. Getting enough sleep plays a crucial role in your emotional state of mind, memory, learning ability, decision making/problem solving and social interaction. Sleep deprivation has been blamed for many bad outcomes including traffic deaths, train accidents, plane crashes and lapses in memory resulting in wrong responses at critical times. If you are not getting enough sleep, your body will not be able to rebuild itself and recharge itself properly. Your body will begin to suffer.

Here are some common symptoms due to lack of sleep:
- Memory loss
- Emotional instability
- Exhaustion, delusions, paranoia, and hallucinations over a prolonged period of sleep deprivation
- Decreased concentration and creativity and disruption in your ability to learn
- Decreased efficiency and productivity; everything seems to require more effort
- Impaired judgment (your priorities and values in life may even change)
- Loss of patience
- Negative changes in your analytical abilities, perception, motivation, and motor control
- Impaired immune system
- Increased feelings of depression, apathy, or irritability and aggression
- Slowed reaction time

On the other hand, getting enough rest and sleep will affect you positively in a number of ways:
- *Memory* – Numerous studies show that a good night's sleep can help improve memory
- *Stress* – There's no better way to dissipate stress than with good old fashioned rest
- *Weight Loss* – People who get adequate sleep every night are more likely to be successful with weight loss
- *Intelligence* – Researchers have discovered that taking a short nap during the day will help you feel refreshed while bolstering intelligence.[7]

Achieving a life of prosperity requires focus, concentration and commitment. In order to achieve this lifestyle you must obtain adequate sleep and rest. This is not something that you can skip or compromise when applying the keys outlined in this book.

---

7 http://www.sciencedaily.com/releases/2005/06/050629070337.htm

102

How Much Sleep Do We Need?

There have been numerous studies and research on sleep and how much sleep an individual needs in order to be effective both mentally and physically. Although there is really no magic number, professionals have determined a healthy range for sleep needs based on a person's age.

How Much Sleep Do You Really Need?[8]

Age	Sleep Needs
Newborns (0 to 2 months)	12-18 hours
Infants (3 to 11 months)	14 to 15 hours
Toddlers (1 to 3 years)	12 to 14 hours
Preschoolers (3 to 5 years)	11 to 13 hours
School-age children (5 to 10 years)	10 to 11 hours
Teens (10 to 17)	8.5 to 9.25 hours
Adults	7 to 9 hours

Compare your current sleep behavior to the above chart. Are you getting enough sleep? If not, adjust your schedule to achieve success in this area.

Why Rest is Important

Although rest and sleep are seen as the same thing, rest does not necessarily mean sleep. Rest consists of the breaks you take (or fail to take) at work during the day, resting prior to and after engaging in stressful activities, or at anytime your body tells you that it is tired and needs a break. Rest can also include restful activities such as reading a book or just closing your eyes and meditating for a short while.

Mental rest and relaxation are often overlooked or discounted as we focus so much on resting our body. You may feel as if you

---

8 National Sleep Foundation, www.sleepfoundation.org

don't have enough time to just sit in a chair and close your eyes for a short period of time. If you have never tried it you will not be able to fully understand its impact. Sometimes we spend time at physical rest but our minds are busy with the stressors of life. This can result in more stress and more physical strain on your body resulting in no real benefit to you.

Allowing your mind to be free from the thoughts of life, to actually "rest" just as you rest your body, will have just as much impact as physical rest. Further, allowing your mind to worry or stress while your body is at rest will counteract that rest. Breathing is a major component to rest. It allows you to control your body and the amount of oxygen that flows to your brain. It increases your body's ability to relax and become at ease.

> "The best cure for the body is a quiet mind."
> —Napoleon Bonaparte

By reviewing the chart on page 103, it is clear that a **lack of rest and sleep is not good for your health, happiness, or success!** Getting enough rest and sleep is an important business decision!

Live the Life You Want Your Children to Model

When it comes to living a life of prosperity, the health and wellness habits you demonstrate will be picked up by your children at a very early age. So expect to see whatever behaviors you display mirrored in your children — good or bad. The old saying, "Do as I say, not as I do," doesn't work. You can't just talk the talk; you must also walk the walk.

In fact, take a quick walk down memory lane right now and recall moments from your own childhood. Did you shadow your parents or a sibling every chance you had? Did you want to do what they were doing? Did you mimic mannerisms or things they said? Even rebellious teenagers discover as adults that they grew up to be "just like my dad," or "just like my mom."

Our influence on our children's lives, though it sometimes seems subtle, is paramount to their development. Whatever children "live" they reflect back to the world. If they live with criticism, they learn to condemn; if they live with shame, they learn to feel guilty;

if they live with encouragement, they learn confidence; if they live with praise, they learn to appreciate; if they live with fairness, they learn justice. And, if they live with health-conscious parents, they learn to be health conscious, too.

In February 2010, the first lady of the United States, Michelle Obama, chose childhood obesity as a cause she wanted to champion. Childhood obesity in the U.S. is now at epidemic proportions.

Unhealthy children can quickly become a drain on the family's bottom line. Days missed from school will cause you to miss work, co-pays to see your family physician and any surgical procedures that may be required will negatively impact your bottom line; or even worse, contribute to your being pushed into bankruptcy.

In addition to financial challenges for you, unhealthy children face personal challenges of their own. Low self-esteem, being teased or bullied at school, depression, eating disorders, and withdrawing from society — these can all result from unhealthy habits. Suddenly the financial strain pales in comparison to the pain you see in your child's eyes.

This trend can be reversed and it all begins with you.

I have a beautiful ten-year-old daughter named Leah; together we walk around the lake, bike, and enjoy healthy meals. In school, she has learned to read product labels to help her make healthy food choices. She takes a good multi vitamin every day. We talk often about the importance of healthy living and make it a part of our family commitment.

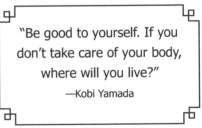

"Be good to yourself. If you don't take care of your body, where will you live?"

—Kobi Yamada

These are small things that have a big impact. You can empower your children to make smart and informed health choices by being a willing participant — and role model.

Unhealthy children grow into unhealthy adults. Don't let this happen to your family. Give your children a jump start to living their own prosperous lives.

A healthy life leads to a successful life. Here are some ways to jumpstart your healthy lifestyle and start you on your way to living a life of prosperity.

How to Jumpstart Your Healthy Lifestyle	
Exercise	**Diet**
Decide that you want to change • Ask yourself what you want to accomplish, i.e., I want to lose weight to possibly prevent illness. • I want to feel better about myself by fitting into old clothes, etc.	Remember. it's not just a "diet." It's a lifestyle change • Changing eating habits takes time so make gradual changes. • Don't restrict yourself from the foods you like, just learn how to cook the same things in a healthier fashion, and control your portion size.
Take it one day at a time • Rome wasn't built in a day. Building your exercise routine won't be either. • Gradual change has a better chance of developing into a lifetime habit.	Get a physical exam and health assessment • Learn what your current health situation is, i.e., what is your blood pressure reading, what are your cholesterol levels, Vitamin D levels, etc. • Learn your optimal statistics, i.e., weight, blood pressure, cholesterol levels • Ask your health care provider questions, no matter how scary you think the answer may be. You need to be knowledgeable about your health in order to make better decisions.
Learn how to exercise • The library has books on exercises, including the use of weights • Find out what exercises you "like" doing • Enlist the services of a personal trainer • Establish a time of day when you can exercise free of distractions. (Most experts recommend first thing in the morning.)	Learn about foods and what vitamins and nutrients they provide • Use the Food Guide Pyramid • Begin moving away from processed foods (foods that have been altered from their original state). • Eat organic foods whenever possible
Find someone you identify with (your exercise role model) • Seek a role model or a person who has been successful in the area of exercise and health (health & wellness mentor) • Learn what they did and continue to do, and then pattern your exercise regimen after his/hers.	Find someone you identify with (your health & wellness role model) • Seek a person who has changed his/her life by changing his/her diet; learn how he/she became successful at it. • Follow your role model if possible through blogs or other means of social media.

✂ Key Principle #4 ✂

Health & Wellness

Maintain a healthy mind, body and spirit.

Why work hard in life and not be able to enjoy it?

Chapter 5

Key Principle #5

Stress, Pressure & Change

Stress, Pressure & Change (Dealing with the Unexpected)

=

Crisis Management

The Life Is A Business! ™
Blueprint To Prosperity

"Many companies have long contended that stress in the home causes productivity loss in the marketplace. And it does. But research now reveals that stress on the job causes stress at home. In other words, they feed off each other."

— Zig Ziglar, Author, Salesperson, Motivational Speaker

Case Study

Johnson & Johnson

Johnson & Johnson CEO:	William Weldon
Number of Employees:	115,000
Fortune 500 Ranking:	#33
Industry:	Medical & Toiletries Manufacturing
Location:	New Brunswick, NJ
Annual Revenue:	$61.8B

It's nearly impossible to get well without Johnson & Johnson (J&J). The diversified health care giant operates in three segments through more than 250 operating companies located in some 60 countries. Its pharmaceuticals division makes drugs for an array of ailments, such as neurological conditions, blood disorders, autoimmune diseases, and pain. Top sellers are psoriasis drug Remicade and schizophrenia medication Risperdal. J&J's medical devices and diagnostics division offers surgical equipment, monitoring devices, orthopedic products, and contact lenses, among other things. Its consumer segment makes over-the-counter drugs and products for baby, skin, and oral care, as well as first aid and women's health.[1]

The gold standard for corporate crisis management remains Johnson & Johnson's response to the Tylenol scare in 1982. Seven people were killed after a murderous lunatic placed cyanide-laced capsules in packages on store shelves. Although the deaths were limited to the Chicago area, J&J immediately recalled all Tylenol nationwide — 31 million bottles — at a cost of about $100 million. The company also launched a public-awareness campaign to protect consumers.[2] Each of J &J operating companies and facilities have implemented a Business Continuity Plan (BCP) to ensure that employees, facilities and products remain safe and secure, and the ability to serve customers remain uninterrupted. BCP maintains a state of preparedness for disruptive events, natural or manmade.[3]

---

1 www.hoovers.com
2 www.I-sight.com
3 Johnson & Johnson 2007 Sustainability report

⤷ Calming the Chaos ⤶

In contrast to J&J's immediate and swift response to crisis, the 2010 Deepwater Horizon oil spill—also referred to as the BP oil spill—in the Gulf of Mexico is a current example of a company without crisis planning. On April 20, 2010, an explosion on the Deepwater Horizon drilling rig killed 11 men working on the platform and injured 17 others. It also started a sea-floor oil gusher, releasing 2.2 million gallons of crude oil PER DAY into the Gulf. BP officials scrambled for 87 days like a chicken with its head cut off trying to come up with a solution to cap the wellhead. The situation was utter chaos. Even after being "fixed," there remains immeasurable damage to marine and wildlife habitats and economic stress from the shutting down of the Gulf's fishing and tourism industries.

Both the J&J and BP disasters were unexpected events. We have unexpected events happen in our lives, too. I have never known anyone who could forecast their car engine blowing out, a sick kid that keeps them home from work for a week, or the surprise ceiling leak that requires the entire roof be replaced. But these types of things can and will happen to each and every one of us. The question then becomes, how prepared are you mentally, spiritually and financially to weather this storm—and calm the chaos—when it comes?

BP's advantage was that, even without a crisis plan, the company had billions of dollars in the bank and enough cash reserves to manage its way through that crisis and take steps to rebuild its reputation. Do you have the reserves to manage your way through a potential crisis?

What is a Crisis?

The simple definition of a crisis is: *a critical event or point of decision which, if not handled, may have catastrophic consequences.* Three common elements of a business crisis are: 1) the event is a threat to the organization, 2) the event is unexpected, and 3) decisions on what to do and how to do it must be made quickly.

Some make the distinction between a crisis and a disaster by defining a disaster as an event that results in great damage, difficulty, or death and that failing to handle a disaster can lead to a crisis. Clearly, the events mentioned previously for J&J and BP reached crisis stage of epic proportions. Hurricane Katrina, 9/11, and so many other tragic events in history were all undeniable crises. Whether you identify an event as a disaster or a crisis, they're both bad.

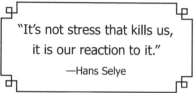

"It's not stress that kills us, it is our reaction to it."
—Hans Selye

What constitutes a crisis in *your* life?

Comparatively, the elements of a life crisis are similar to a company crisis.

Components of a Crisis	
Fortune 500 Company	**Your Prosperous Life**
The event is a threat to the security and success of the organization	The event is a threat to the safety and security of you and your family
The event is unexpected	The event is unexpected
Decisions must be made quickly	Decisions must be made quickly

The scale of impact may be smaller than a J&J or BP disaster, but personal crisis is no less damaging for individuals. Unexpected events that add stress, drain finances, heighten emotions, and chip away at your sense of security can all be considered a personal crisis. Things like: your spouse dying from injuries suffered in a car accident, your child being diagnosed with a long-term or life-threatening illness, your employer downsizes and you lose your job, or your house is severely damaged from a house fire—during which you lose most of your possessions. All of these unforeseen tragedies reach a critical "point of decision" on what to do next and how to get through it.

Stress, Pressure and Change

Tragic events are not the only catalysts for crisis. High degrees of stress, ongoing pressures, and change — good or bad — can disrupt your life and, if not managed, create chaos and escalate to bigger problems and challenges. For example, getting married, having a baby, buying a new car, sending a child to college, moving to a new home — these are all "good" changes that disrupt our lives. Each of them brings added stress, both emotionally and financially. If we are not prepared to take on the additional responsibility, these good changes could trigger bad results.

Stress and pressure are not always bad. Sometimes a little pressure motivates us or makes us realize that we need to make a positive change to avoid something negative happening in our life. However, heightened stress and pressure can cause us to panic, it can cause us to behave in ways that we would not normally behave and may even cause us to make poor decisions that worsen the situation. Stress can also cause health problems, both physical and mental.

How to Work Through a Crisis

I want to start this section by discussing what types of events are not crises. A flat tire on your car is not a crisis. Locking your keys in your house is not a crisis. Cutting your finger and needing three stitches is not a crisis. Your son falling off his bike and getting a knot on his head is usually not a crisis. These things are just a part of life and shouldn't create the type of response that an actual crisis could. Learn how to differentiate a crisis from a non-crisis to decrease unnecessary stress and anxiety.

Although it is nearly impossible to prevent stress or disastrous events from occurring in our lives, you can prepare for the unthinkable. Developing a plan minimizes the potentially heavy toll they take both financially and emotionally. Anything that helps reduce your stress, lessen your anxiety, relieve the pressure, or cope with change when the unexpected strikes, will allow you to take action quickly, calm the chaos, and work through the situation with a level head.

In business, companies focus on creating two distinct plans: risk management and crisis management. Although closely related, they are not the same. Risk management deals with assessing potential threats and identifying the best ways to *avoid* those threats. Crisis management involves dealing with threats *after* they occur and minimize the damage. It is critical for a company to be prepared for both if it is to survive.

Corporations put plans into place that address varied and complex issues. In addition to preparing for fire, safety, and emergency procedures, most companies also prepare for things like an abrupt drop in stock values, employee misconduct, product liability claims, equipment malfunction, cyber threats and strained community relations.

How people react when faced with a crisis is crucial in determining how well the company comes out of it. The CEO's behavior will be closely watched by all. Will he or she fall apart or lead in a cool, calm, collected and confident way? The goal of developing a plan is to ensure that employees and managers have the right tools available to get the crisis under control, and do it as quickly as possible to minimize damage.

Let's take a quick look at our case study company, Johnson & Johnson, and why I chose this company to lead this chapter. Prior to the Tylenol scare, the company could not possibly anticipate someone's devious plot to murder unsuspecting people by replacing Tylenol capsules with cyanide-laced capsules and putting them on store shelves. Yet, the company's action to remove ALL Tylenol from store shelves — even though this only occurred in the Chicago area — came quickly and probably prevented a greater number of additional tragedies.

What the company was prepared for, however, is the associated costs with this action. The company's risk management planning included insurance to cover possible losses, and liquid cash reserves that were adequate to cover anything that the insurance did not. This cash reserve is the corporate equivalent of a rainy day fund. Because of this planning, the Tylenol tragedy did not result in a second tragedy of wiping out the business.

115

Fortune 500 Companies go to great lengths to prepare themselves for the unexpected; we, too, should prepare our life's business in the same way, planning ahead for ways to *avoid* threats of disaster, and having safeguards in place to deal with threats *after* they occur.

Crisis Prevention

You have already begun to use crisis prevention planning by reading this book. Further, you have begun to put into place, or at least thought about, ways to put yourself in the position of preventing life's stressors. Let's review:

Strategic Plan – Key Principle #2: We discussed the importance of having a road map for your life, which includes the goals and tasks necessary to accomplish your vision (Key Principle #1). Having a strategic plan forces you to address possible "weaknesses" and "threats" that may negatively impact achieving your vision. These threats can potentially cause us stress or place pressure on our lives. Having a solid strategic plan that allows you to identify possible life stressors in advance will also allow you to "hedge" against these issues, reducing the likelihood that they will negatively impact your stress levels and bottom line.

Financial Planning – Key Principle #3: Financial planning helps us properly plan for unexpected events. We will discuss the importance of having cash reserves later in this chapter. However, if you review the basics of Key Principle #3, it is important to know where your money is spent each month so that you can build cash reserves and avoid over draft fees that catch you unprepared for life's unexpected financial stressors.

Health & Wellness – Key Principle #4: You learned the importance of health and wellness and became aware of the financial impact of poor health habits, i.e. being sick, needing medication, missing work, etc. Loss of work due to short-term illness, chronic illness and fatigue significantly induces stress. The healthier you are the more likely you will be able to avoid stress associated with poor health, increased healthcare expenses and loss of work.

Your Preparedness Plan

So, what can you actually DO to prevent or minimize adverse effects of a crisis in your life?

Glad you asked!

Like Fortune 500 Companies, you must plan for the unexpected in your quest for a life to prosperity. If you are married or have a family, involve everyone in the planning and assign specific tasks for each family member to do. Here are three top priorities for your preparedness plan.

Increase Awareness

Many of us live our lives, day by day, taking what comes and dealing with it on the spot. We think that we are good "life" managers and have the wherewithal to make quick decisions on key issues. Don't kid yourself. By its very nature, a crisis can be overwhelming and the old adage, "failing to plan is planning to fail," rings true in times of crisis.

A good practice to increase awareness is to gather your family members together and play the "what if" game. Even young children can participate. Ask each person to share their biggest worries. The "big" ones might include job loss, a house fire, long-term illness or devastating injury, and death. Children may tell you it's getting lost, missing the bus to get home from school,

> "How we perceive a situation and how we react to it is the basis of our stress. If you focus on the negative in any situation, you can expect high stress levels. However, if you try and see the good in the situation, your stress levels will greatly diminish."
> —Catherine Pulsifer, My Story

or being bullied. If the event causes fear, stress, or anxiety, it is a valid potential crisis for that individual.

Once you've detailed your potential crisis, ask and answer "what if" that happened? What could we do about it? How should we deal with it? What could we do now that would help to make it less scary if it happened? Is there anything that could be done to prevent it from happening at all?

Increasing awareness of what could happen, and then talking about how to diminish the long-term effects if it does, increases the feeling of security that you and your family members need.

Be Prepared

Boy Scouts learn to live by the organization's motto of "Be Prepared." It's good advice for all of us. Being prepared for unforeseen crisis is usually tied to pursuing and securing protection "just in case" something happens. These protections help to alleviate both financial and emotional burdens that arise along with the crisis.

Insurance is front and center when it comes to being prepared. Basically, when you purchase insurance, you are paying to transfer the risk of significant loss or damage to another. That sounds like a pretty good deal, don't you think? You are protecting yourself from large financial losses by paying a relatively small premium. Life insurance (for all family members), home insurance, health insurance (for all family members), car insurance—these are all protections against potentially huge financial burdens in times of crisis. One car accident that leads to a legal battle, a fire that burns your house to the ground, or the loss of a spouse could completely wipe you out both emotionally and financially.

People tend to complain about costs and think in terms of "I'm paying for something that may never happen," instead of "I'm protecting my family and my assets." They feel like they are just throwing their money away if they don't get something tangible in return. Look at it this way: if you get to the end of your life and never had to cash in on any of your insurance policies, you'll have had a far more fortunate, stress-free, happy life than if you had to face a devastating crisis where you did have to rely on insurance. That's worth more than all the money you collectively pay out in premiums.

Short and Long Term Disability

During a recent conversation with a friend, she recalled taking a new position out of law school. She had accumulated little vacation time or sick leave and was suddenly faced with an unplanned pregnancy. Her supervisor asked her if she was enrolled in the short term disability program offered through the company's human resources. My friend was slightly embarrassed that she did not know what short term disability was, but even more embarrassed to admit that, except for health insurance, she quickly skipped over every benefit listed without investigating them.

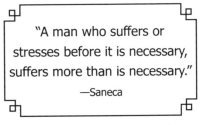

"A man who suffers or stresses before it is necessary, suffers more than is necessary."
—Saneca

I was a little perplexed, given that I was speaking with a woman who had recently graduated from law school, but I asked the golden question, "Why?" She responded, "Money." Fortunately she took her supervisor's advice, inquired about short term disability, and learned that the cost was $16 per pay period. After she had the baby, she received 8 weeks of leave and $252.00 in benefits per pay period. It cost her approximately .06 cent for each $1.00 of benefits she received. This was a "business decision" she was glad she made. Without this money she would have taken unpaid leave and either used the small amount of money she had saved or applied for some form of government assistance. Either way the result would have caused undue stress and pressure at a time that should have been joyful.

The *Will*—a "must have" in your arsenal of protective paperwork—seems to be one thing people regularly put off preparing. Understandably, it's a little frightening to plan for your death. Yet, more than any other disaster, it is the one thing we know is inevitable. Death is one of the most catastrophic events a family will experience. For some, it is financially devastating, and for all, it is emotionally devastating.

A **will** or **testament** is a legal declaration by which a person, the testator, names one or more persons to manage his/her estate and provides for the transfer of his/her property at death.

119

Having life insurance is a start but it is not enough. While life insurance will help your family pay for expenses and provide financial support for their future, it does not help them carry out your wishes. Preparing a will allows you to specify the management and distribution of your estate after your death. In the absence of a will, your family is left to sort through your estate and determine who gets what, and under what conditions. It is emotionally draining for them, and blatantly irresponsible of you.

Wills are not just for the wealthy who have a lot of "stuff," investments, and bulging coffers of cash. If you have anything that is of value to you — or that would be particularly appreciated by someone you know — the only way to ensure it goes to the person you want to have it is by preparing a will.

Life After Death

In the unlikely/untimely event of the death of a corporate CEO, the business must go on; the business doesn't die because its leader did. This is true with the business of our lives.

Anna Nicole Smith became a tabloid sensation when she married Texas oil billionaire J. Howard Marshall in 1994. Fourteen months later, Marshall passed away, leaving his estimated $1.6 billion estate to his son – instead of Smith. Smith later sued Marshall's son, E. Pierce Marshall, for $300 million, the amount that Smith claimed her late husband promised her. The court originally ruled in her favor, but in an appeal, a court reversed the ruling and upheld the reversal in March 2010. Although Marshall passed away in 1995, the business of his life is still up and running. Oh, and let's not forget, Anna Nicole Smith passed away in 2007.

A will, depending on the value of your estate, and your wishes, could be simple to execute, or could require the assistance of a qualified attorney. There are many types of wills, but they all require these components to be considered legal:

1. You must be 18 years of age or an emancipated minor
2. You must be of sound mind
3. You must expressly state that this document is your Will

4. You must have the Will signed ("attested") by at least two or three witnesses
5. You must have substantive provisions that:
   - Nominate a legal guardian for any minor children;
   - List who inherits specific items;
   - State what happens to remaining property (residue) not mentioned in the will
6. You must appoint an executor who will be:
   - Responsible for supervising the distribution of property;
   - Responsible for paying all of your debts and taxes;

Other types of wills include:
   - A Simple Will provides for the outright distribution of assets for an uncomplicated estate.
   - A Holographic or Handwritten Will is prepared in your own handwriting.
   - A Pour-Over Will "pours over" –or transfers--property into a Trust when you die.
   - A Joint Will is one made by two people, each leaving all of their property and assets to the other.
   - An Attorney Prepared Will prepared and individually designed for you by a professional attorney.

A research study published in 2007 found that for the last three years, 55% of all adult Americans do not have a will. Only one in three African American adults (32 percent) and one in four Hispanic American adults (26 percent) have wills, compared to more than half (52 percent) of white American adults.[1]

In 2006, $255,861 was the average size of insurance policy sold[2] and the average funeral in the United States costs $6,500, according to the National Funeral Directors Association.[3] Simple math tells us there is a large amount of cash left over that will be needed to settle the remaining business of the estate. Do your family a huge favor

1 http://wiki.answers.com
2 www.wholesaleinsurance.net
3 http://articles.moneycentral.msn.com

by developing a will with very specific instructions. While it will not guarantee things will close out smoothly, it certainly increases the chances of avoiding all-too-common family feuds over who gets what.

Build Cash Reserves

Insurance will not cover every crisis that results in financial challenges. For example, if your spouse sustains injuries or long-term illness that prevents him or her from working, insurance may cover medical costs, but will not cover lost wages. For this situation, you need to be prepared with good, old fashioned cash reserves—savings.

In Key Principle #3, we discussed how having a solid financial plan is essential to creating a life of prosperity and to dedicate a separate account to a "crisis fund" that is built up over time. How much is enough? Although great financial minds, authors, and self-proclaimed financial gurus each have an opinion on what constitutes "adequate savings," I recommend you have, at a minimum, a crisis fund containing enough cash to cover total household expenses for one full year. For example, if your monthly expenses are $5,000, your crisis savings account should be no less than $60,000.

> "Stress is not what happens to us., It's our response to what happens. And response is something we can choose."
>
> —Maureen Killoran

Sounds like a lot of money, doesn't it? It is a lot of money, and that's the goal—to have a reserve that you or your family can rely on for a significant length of time if one or both wage earners were to suddenly lose their income. To reach your ultimate goal, start building your reserves with smaller goals. Set a target of three months worth of savings. When you achieve that goal, double it. Keep building until your crisis fund is complete. Remember, the 'crisis' account must be separate from your short-term savings account. Money should never be withdrawn unless you experience a major disaster or crisis and you have no other options.

Ways to build your cash reserve:

- Start saving unexpected money. This could be money received as a birthday gift, money from a tax return, money you may have found, money from something you sold or other income that's not part of your paycheck.
- Seek extra hours at work or get a part time job.
- Resist the temptation to spend on things you don't absolutely need.
- At the end of every day empty all of your loose pocket change into a safe place.

Be creative and come up with other ways that may best suit you.

Other Ways to Plan for Stress, Pressure & Change

Other ways to plan for stress, pressure and change is by taking small preventive measures such as:

- If you own an older model vehicle, an AAA membership is a small but great investment if or when your vehicle stalls or needs a tow.
- Earmark a portion of your vacation time for things such as illness, doctor's appointments, transportation issues or even weather conditions. Doing this is a great way to keep stress and pressure in check when the unexpected but inevitable takes place.
- Keep a first aid kit in your home. How is having a first aid kit on hand considered a business decision? Stress usually affects your bottom line negatively and, in the event of an injury, having a first aid kit will be one less pressure amid the chaos.

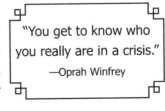

"You get to know who you really are in a crisis."
—Oprah Winfrey

Business decisions can be big or small. Making the wrong decision (or no decision) on what appears to be a small matter could be as devastating as the effects from a big one.

Crises will happen; it's just a part of life's experience. The stress, pressure and change that precede and accompany

123

a crisis can be demoralizing if no provisions are in place. Don't let this be you.

Arming yourself with insurance, a will, and cash reserves is a smart business decision and every successful and prosperous life must include these protections as part of its plan. Our lives and situations are ever-changing, so review and revise your plan each year to make sure your plan still fits your life.

> "When you find yourself stressed, ask yourself one question: Will this matter in 5 years from now? If yes, then do something about the situation. If no, then let it go."
>
> —Catherine Pulsifer

CRISIS MANAGEMENT CHECKLIST

Prevention Checklist

- ____ Strategic Plan

- ____ Health & Wellness Plan

- ____ Strong Financial Plan

Planning Checklist

- ____ Educate Self & Family

- ____ Insurance

- ____ Will

- ____ Cash Reserves

- ____ Misc. Add your personal checklist items

೮⁀ Key Principle #5 ⁀೨

Stress, Pressure & Change: Crisis Management

Prepare for inevitable stress, pressure and change so you
can better manage your way through them.

*Stress, pressure and change happen in all of our lives —
you are not being singled out.*

Chapter 6

Key Principle #6

Stewardship/Philanthropy

Stewardship/Philanthropy

=

Social Responsibility

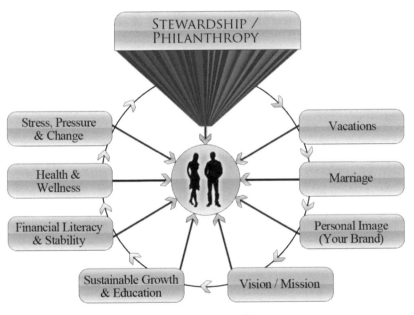

The Life Is A Business! ™
Blueprint To Prosperity

"If service is the rent you pay for your existence on this earth, are you behind in your rent?"

—Robert G. Allen, Author

Case Study

Microsoft

Microsoft CEO:	Steven A. Ballmer
Number of Employees:	93,000
Fortune 500 Ranking:	#36
Industry:	Computer Software
Location:	Redmond, WA
Annual Revenue:	$58.4B

Microsoft's ambitions are anything but small. The world's #1 software company provides a variety of products and services, including its ubiquitous Windows operating systems and Office software suite. Microsoft has expanded into markets such as video game consoles, customer relationship management applications, server and storage software, and digital music players.

The company has also used selective acquisitions to bulk up its presence in markets such as online advertising, mobile devices, and enterprise software. In 2008 Microsoft made repeated efforts to acquire Yahoo! but was ultimately rebuffed; the two companies instead signed a deal in 2009 to combine their search operations.[1]

---

1 www.hoovers.com

What Goes Around Comes Around

Nearly all Fortune 500 Companies embrace business ethics to be socially responsible. While there's no proof that this enhances company profits, I would argue that indirectly it does impact company profits by bolstering the company's image and reputation. The greater the image and reputation, the greater the customer loyalty, which increases consumer purchasing. It will do the same for your business/life.

Few types of activities release endorphins the way giving back to society does. I would argue that a happy employee is more productive and focused than an unhappy employee which ultimately would improve the company's (family's) bottom line.

We all bear the responsibility of being philanthropic. This chapter's case study company, Microsoft, supports numerous programs and activities for the betterment of many communities and groups, including seniors, teens, and nonprofits.[1] Additionally, the company's co-founder, Bill Gates, teamed with his wife, Melinda, to form the Bill and Melinda Gates Foundation. The foundation funds various initiatives worldwide, ranging from educational grants to medical research. In fact, in 2009, the couple donated their entire dividends from Microsoft stock to their foundation--$3 billion.[2]

Clearly this is a significant commitment to make, but there is a misconception surrounding philanthropy. Oftentimes, the people who are publicly touted for their giving are wealthy, i.e. Bill and Melinda Gates, Warren Buffett and most recently Mark Zuckerberg (Facebook founder). Mr. Zuckerberg donated one hundred million dollars to the City of New Jersey's school district. For this reason many of us feel like we can't be a philanthropist because we aren't wealthy, but that couldn't be further from the truth.

---

1 http://www.microsoft.com/hk/giving/caprogram/default.mspx
2 http://www.toptenz.net/top-10-philanthropists.php

Philanthropy is a Greek term which means "love of mankind." Philanthropy is an idea, event, or action that is done to better humanity and usually involves some "sacrifice" as opposed to being done for a profit motive. Acts of philanthropy include donating money to a charity, volunteering at a local shelter, or raising money to donate to cancer research. **Nowhere does it say you have to be wealthy!**

> "The true measure of a man is how much he gives when he has little, not how much he gives when he has a lot."
> —Charles E. Cox, Jr.

Why is philanthropy a key to living a Prosperous Life?

There are several reasons why philanthropy is one of the nine keys to living and managing a prosperous life. In general, your "success" in life is not only measured by what you do for a living, your role in society, your income or your status. It has as much to do with your impact, socially as well as financially, on the community in which you live and the world at large. There are five definite reasons why philanthropy and social responsibility are crucial to living a prosperous life: (1) It feels good, (2) It strengthens community (3) It is directly connected to and impacts Key Principle # 9: Brand, which is your reputation (4) Opportunity to Network and (5) Positive Generational Impact.

It Feels Good

We have to admit that there is something a little selfish about being socially responsible, and there is nothing wrong with that. You cannot deny that when you help someone or volunteer in a community organization, you just plain feel good, that's the way God designed it.

Feeling good about doing good is a very natural result for human beings. Volunteering provides physical and mental rewards including reducing stress. Experts report that when you focus on someone other than yourself it interrupts the usual pattern of stress.

Feeling good increases your overall mental and physical health, which allows you to function more effectively in society.

When I first began volunteering at Bethesda Hospital in Saint Paul, Minnesota in 2009, I quickly began to feel the positive effects from this. I was at a period in my life where it seemed everything was bad and that the world was against me. My responsibilities at Bethesda quickly took my mind off of myself, and placed it on the patients, who had far more challenges to overcome than I could have ever imagined.

My responsibilities included just talking to the patients or their family members. Empathy, which I didn't even know I had, quickly kicked in. When it did, it created a type of euphoria that's difficult to describe. I slowly began to notice that I was smiling more, and with the help of the patients that I was there to console, began to see my posture restored. Through volunteering I was slowly being healed.

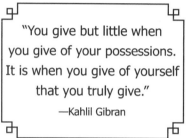

"You give but little when you give of your possessions. It is when you give of yourself that you truly give."

—Kahlil Gibran

Things eventually got better for me and I became too busy to continue that commitment. Then one day I got a call from Bethesda. The lady on the other end said she was asked to call me. She said that there was a paid part time position available and they thought I would be a perfect fit for it. I interviewed, was offered the position and accepted it. I thanked them for the opportunity and told them I would have done it for free. I am still proudly a part time staff member there. I once read that **"It is more blessed to give than to receive."** This was proving to be true in my life.

The euphoria the body receives is organic, it's a unique type of high that no synthetic chemical will ever be able to provide, this high has no artificial ingredients.

Michael Steger, a psychologist at the University of Louisville in Kentucky, conducted a study to determine which behavior makes people happier: seeking pleasure or doing good? He asked a group of 65 undergraduates to complete an online survey each day for three weeks that assessed how many times they participated in pleasure-seeking behaviors, versus meaningful activities, such as helping others, listening to friends' problems and/or pursuing one's life goals.

The surveys asked the subjects how much purpose they felt their lives had each day and whether they felt happy or sad. The subjects also completed two sets of questionnaires at the beginning and end of the study to assess how they felt about their lives more generally. They found that the more people participated in meaningful activities, the happier they were and the more purposeful their lives felt. Pleasure-seeking behaviors, on the other hand, did not make people happier. Realizing that some people may feel guilty about reporting pleasure-seeking behaviors, Steger and his colleagues then modified the survey questions slightly to make them seem less objectionable, and asked a new group of students to perform the study again, this time over a four-week period. The psychologists got the same results.[3]

I think the story of Pat Tillman, an NFL recruit who gave up his career to serve in the U.S. Army, is a true example of how sometimes "good" trumps what we may think as good for us. Pat Tillman was a football standout but was far from a household name when he put aside his NFL career to enlist in the U.S. Army.

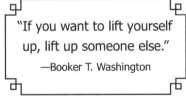

"If you want to lift yourself up, lift up someone else."
—Booker T. Washington

Tillman had married his high school sweetheart and had been offered a $3.6 million contract extension by the Arizona Cardinals when he enlisted in the Army. At first thought, even I say, "Why would you give up $3.6 million over going to war?" According to Tillman, he was moved by the 9/11 attacks. Tillman wanted to serve his country. Even further, Tillman refused to publically discuss his decision because he did not feel that he was doing anything different than any other solider who enlisted. Tillman died serving his country. Although he died at the hands of his fellow soldiers in what has been deemed an accident, the fact remains, he gave up what was clearly good for him, for what he thought would be good for others.

---

3 http://www.livescience.com/health/070503_doing_good.html

It may seem contrary to what we are taught in society but doing for others gets us much farther in life than doing for ourselves. It benefits us emotionally and physically. Feeling good helps us to achieve our vision in life. In addition to the emotional benefits, there are also physical benefits.

The Corporation for National and Community Services funded research to determine the link between volunteerism and health. In general, research found that "there is a strong relationship between volunteering and health: those who volunteer have lower mortality rates, greater functional ability, and lower rates of depression later in life than those who do not volunteer.

Comparisons of the health benefits of volunteering for different age groups have also shown that older volunteers are the most likely to receive greater benefits from volunteering, whether it is because they are more likely to face higher incidence of illness or because volunteering provides them with physical and social activity and a sense of purpose at a time when their social roles are changing. Some of these findings also indicate that volunteers who devote a "considerable" amount of time to volunteer activities (about 100 hours per year) are most likely to exhibit positive health outcomes."[4]

Strengthens Community

There is no questioning the fact that volunteering is a great way to pull people together and build stronger communities. We have seen time and time again the impact of volunteering when tragedy hits a community. A perfect example is the earthquake that recently devastated Port-au-Prince, Haiti. People from the hip hop community to the Red Cross to the NBA and everyone in between rolled up their sleeves to help. There is little doubt that without the efforts of these individuals and organizations, Haiti would not have seen the amount of food and water delivered, or the quick rebuilding of its communities.

Countless other individuals, just like you and me, gave small amounts of money to provide relief. Other people with specialized

4 http://www.nationalservice.gov/pdf/07_0506_hbr.pdf

talents and skills like doctors, carpenters and teachers left the comfort of their homes to assist the victims. These people were not "rich" in terms of money like the more recognizable athletes and entertainers. They were people who saw a need and decided to do their part. I have no doubt that these individuals lead fulfilled lives because of their philanthropic actions.

Growing up in Minnesota, I have been a witness to this kind of generosity often. As you have probably heard, it snows a lot here. When it snows, people with shovels, snow blowers and plow trucks all work together to make everyone safe, and to get everyone back on the road. In the dead of winter you will see people bundled up but with a smile, as they are helping a total stranger. It's this type of activity that helps make the world community stronger. It's this type of behavior, attitude and action that builds and sustains communities.

Volunteering is also a way to take financial strains off of communities. There is constant talk these days about budget cuts and deficit reduction. Kids of all ages are aware of the fact that our country is "in the red". One way we can pull out of this is through volunteering, through our philanthropic mindset. With the cuts

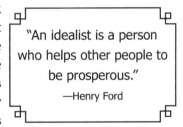

"An idealist is a person who helps other people to be prosperous."
—Henry Ford

in funding of community programs, it is imperative that everyday people like you and me become active and take ownership of our communities.

When programs lose money to fund activities, they survive on volunteers. When programs are completely shut down, people with the ability must step forward to fill the gap. There are things, talents if you will, that we all possess. Some of us have experience that is needed in our communities such as teachers, attorneys and carpenters. Some of us have time to give because our current situation allows. Some are able to contribute financially to programs. Some of us even have the ability to envision and create programs that strengthen community. With just a small time commitment you could help ease the community shortfalls.

Here is a short list of some of the ways you can help strengthen your community:

- Support families (daycare and elder care)
- Support schools (tutoring, classroom support, chaperoning, attending school board meetings)
- Support youth (mentoring, and after-school activities)
- Beautify the community (neighborhood clean ups, tree planting)
- Attend neighborhood group meetings (sit on the board)
- Attend city council meetings or run for public office even if there is no salary attached to the position.

Most of these things don't cost anything more than a small amount of your time and/or talent. Through volunteering, people have been known to find their hidden talents and passion about things they never knew existed. There are also more subtle ways to contribute that are equally as important:

- Help family members who are less fortunate than you
- Donate used clothing, household goods and appliances to charities or local community thrift stores
- Listen to someone who needs someone to talk to
- Smile and say hello to everyone you see, even when you don't feel like smiling

I am proud to report that at the time of the printing of this book, Minnesota is the #3 state for volunteerism and the city I live in, Minneapolis, is the #1 city in the U.S. for volunteerism, according to the Corporation for National and Community Service.[5]

Top 5 States for Volunteer Rate

1. Utah
2. Iowa
3. Minnesota
4. Nebraska
5. Alaska

---

5 www.volunteeringinamerica.gov

Top 5 Large Cities for Volunteer Rate
1.   Minneapolis-St. Paul, MN
2.   Portland, OR
3.   Salt Lake City, UT
4.   Seattle, WA
5.   Oklahoma City, OK

According to the Corporation for National and Community Service, volunteerism is on the rise. The top areas for volunteering are religious and educational organizations, making up over 60%. As you can see from the chart below, there are numerous ways to volunteer. In 2009, 63.4 million people contributed 8.1 billion hours of their time equaling an estimated dollar value of approximately $169 billion for their services.

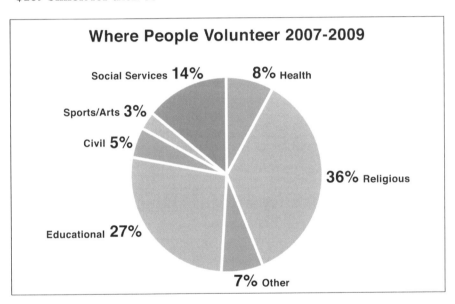

Imagine the loss if all of these people cut their volunteer time in half. Imagine if the government or tax payers had to actually "fund" the loss of volunteer hours, $169 billion worth. It is clear that volunteerism is necessary, if not a must, to strengthening community. In the beginning of this chapter you may have had doubts about volunteering being a business decision but, with the dollar amounts being in the billions, you should be convinced by now that it is.

Assist With Defining Your Brand

The most gratifying way to build or re-build your brand is through your stewardship. People naturally gravitate to sincere goodwill. People who enjoy assisting those less fortunate seem to have a certain aura about them, a glow that precedes them. This type of community service can rebuild a reputation that has taken a beating or take an already good reputation and make it great. If you want you and your family's brand to be associated with goodwill, stewardship and service, there's no easier way to establish that than through volunteering.

General Mills Corporation partnered with "The Biggest Loser" for many reasons and I would bet one of them is to enhance its brand. Company leaders know the importance of demonstrating, through action, their sincerity regarding the health and wellness of their employees as well as the community they serve.

We have all driven an interstate highway and seen "adopt a highway" signs. The idea is for a business to adopt a section of the highway and be responsible for maintaining the cleanliness of it— and sometimes even take on beautification projects. The employees typically volunteer to be a part of the in-house team. These employees are able to accomplish several things by doing this but two of the most obvious ones are:
- Employees gain favor from the higher-ups (their internal brand is being cultivated)
- They return to work and eventually home having had an enormous endorphin release

Again, all it costs is some of your time and talent.

Combining Volunteering and Networking

Volunteering is a great avenue for advancing your professional career. You will be rubbing elbows with people from many different walks of life. Those persons' connections could easily become your connection. It exposes you to people who will learn of your skills and may know where they would be useful.

Volunteering often will give you access to people you might not otherwise be able to access and it indirectly shows people your ability to take initiative to do what's right.

Volunteering also looks good on your résumé or biography. Volunteering feels good to the person doing it, but also impresses the person who learns of your unselfish efforts.

I have a dear friend who is an electrician. I was sharing with him some of the things I was involved with surrounding philanthropy and I instantly noticed a difference in his mannerism. He said he felt he needed to get involved with some of these things. I could see him reflecting on his life, and how fortunate he has been. Before we finished talking, he gave me his email address and asked me to keep him  apprised of any opportunity for him to participate. He probably had no idea of the opportunity this will present for him to network; he was approaching this from a truly altruistic standpoint. And there's nothing wrong with that!

> "There are those who give with joy, and that joy is their reward."
> —Khalil Gibran

Below are some suggestions for getting yourself started with volunteering:

- Think of causes that are near and dear to your heart (cancer research, diabetes research, homelessness, etc.)
- Look for volunteer opportunities that match your skills
- Seek out new experiences that may provide more skills or connections
- Invite a friend to join you and identify charities you can support together

Positive Generational Impact

Volunteering is a staple in all Fortune 500 Companies and transcends CEOs, CFOs and board members. These companies take

social responsibility seriously, no matter the economic outlook. It's this kind if stewardship that lifts spirits during tough times and maintains morale in good times. This too is a characteristic that should be taken seriously in your personal life and handed down through generations. The value of this type of service is immeasurable.

Many well-known families have made volunteering the family moniker. But many more unknown families embrace volunteering as a life value instilled at a young age. At Bethesda Hospital in St. Paul, I work with a young lady named Emily. I was told of her family's history of volunteering at Bethesda and I wanted to hear more, so I asked if she would sit down with me to talk about it. She explained to me that, as a kid, she was encouraged by her parents to volunteer. She recalled coming to the hospital at a young age (her mom is a nurse there) and wanting to volunteer in the gift shop. What makes this story remarkable is that her three older siblings at some point also volunteered at Bethesda and all eventually became paid employees. I asked if they were forced and she replied, no. Her parents clearly did a good job explaining the importance of volunteering to their children, which made them want to do it.

Clearly this was part of the family's overall vision. I suspect if you ask them how they would feel if they were told they couldn't serve others, the mere thought might move them to tears. Below are a few of the benefits of family volunteerism:

- Children are able to develop compassion for and an understanding of others.
- Parents can lead by example while spending time with their kids, pass on important values, and have intimate dialogue in a positive environment.
- Society benefits because children taught volunteering are more likely to volunteer as an adult.

As of the writing of this book, the United States deficit is more than $14 trillion. I feel as though volunteering is one way we can all band together to help bring this number in line. As a country, if we began volunteering in our public schools, our local public works departments, and began keeping the neighborhoods in which we live free from litter and graffiti, these small things could lift some of the burden off our federal, state and local governments.

Volunteering is also a great way for all of us to keep things in perspective. When things are bad and it feels like the world is against us, volunteering can be a great reminder that no matter how bad things might seem, they could always be worse.

Philanthropy is a Key Principle to the living and managing your life to prosperity because it strengthens you personally, mentally and spiritually to be a better person and a better manager of your business…your life.

∾ Key Principle #6 ∾

Stewardship/Philanthropy

Serve your community to build a sense of community.

When you help others elevate their self-worth,
you learn more than you teach.

Chapter 7

Key Principle #7

Vacations

Vacations

=

Fringe Benefits

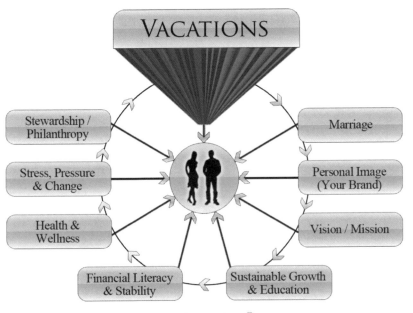

VACATIONS

Stewardship / Philanthropy

Marriage

Stress, Pressure & Change

Personal Image (Your Brand)

Health & Wellness

Vision / Mission

Financial Literacy & Stability

Sustainable Growth & Education

The Life Is A Business! ™
Blueprint To Prosperity

"A vacation is what you take when you can no longer take what you've been taking."

—Earl Wilson, American journalist, author and columnist

Case Study

Intel

Intel CEO:	Paul S. Otellini
Number of Employees:	79,800
Fortune 500 Ranking:	#62
Industry:	Technology
Location:	Santa Clara, CA
Annual Revenue:	$31.5B

The intelligence inside your computer could very well be Intel. The company — which holds about 80% of the market share for microprocessors that go into desktop and notebook computers, and also into computer servers — is still #1 in semiconductors. Archrival AMD ate into Intel's market share for a time, but the big guy fought back with faster processors and advanced manufacturing technology.

Intel also makes embedded semiconductors for the industrial, medical, and in-vehicle infotainment markets. While most computer makers use Intel processors, PC giants Dell and Hewlett-Packard are the company's largest customers. The Asia/Pacific region generates about two-thirds of Intel's revenues.[1]

---

1 www.hoovers.com

Rest, Recharge, Re-focus

Intel has taken the importance of vacations for its employees to a new level by incorporating sabbaticals into its fringe benefit package. A sabbatical, for those who are unfamiliar with the term, is an extended break from your job that gives you time to reflect on your accomplishments, decide how to prioritize your life and career, and is used to de-stress and rest from burn-out so you will return to work rejuvenated. It is often a time to reconnect with family and friends.

A sabbatical lasts for an extended period of time, unlike a typical vacation, which is usually short term. During the sabbatical the employee is completely detached from the job. Sabbaticals, or some variation of them, are becoming increasingly popular with Fortune 500 Companies. They have recognized this as both a way to attract the best worker and then to keep that worker highly effective and motivated. Corporations are clear that giving vacation time is a business decision that positively impacts its bottom line.

I read a headline that said, "Rejuvenate Your Life and Career with a Sabbatical." What struck me most was the fact that going on vacation could enhance both your life and career. I realized, on the spot, that vacationing was a business decision that would affect my bottom line. I am certain that many of you don't consider vacation to be a business decision—oh, but it is.

Vacations serve many purposes for you and your family. The obvious is the opportunity to relax and see things and places you've never seen before. But it doesn't stop there. Vacations give families the opportunity to decompress and re-connect. It's a time to catch up with friends and a time to complete important personal tasks that may have gone overlooked.

The Benefits of Vacations

Vacations stave off burnout, can keep us healthy, strengthen bonds, help with your job performance and are the perfect time to discuss/discover new interests. Frequent vacations lead to increased overall quality of life. These benefits serve as proof that vacations are a business decision. Vacations are also a necessity for children. They also feel stress, peer pressure, and the emotional and physical effects of puberty. Oftentimes adults feel the demands of school work that create similar stress and pressure on children. The more relaxed our children are, the better their academic performance, which in turn can lead to a more optimistic adult life. The result is overall life prosperity.

Fortune 500 Companies see the benefits of vacation time for their employees. Jay Henderson, managing partner for the Chicago office of the worldwide accounting firm of PricewaterhouseCoopers, knows the importance of quality time off. According to a July 2005 article in Bloomberg Business Week[1], Henderson did something he had never done before. He dedicated the content of the entire issue of Chicago Wrap, the bimonthly newsletter he writes and sends to the firm's 1,400 Chicago employees, to the importance of taking a vacation.

The article quotes Henderson as saying, "I thought it was important to focus everyone on the importance of effective vacation experiences." He elaborates, "Vacations can improve the quality of lives and the quality of the professional services we offer if you come back focused and recharged. When I plan my vacations effectively, I'm able to return to work with a strong focus and energy level."[2]

Vacations for employees are clearly important for Fortune 500 Companies. As a business owner, you must take vacations in order to achieve a life of prosperity. Vacations have three important aspects: (1) Rest and Relaxation, (2) Opportunity to Reconnect with Family and Friends, (3) Opportunity to Reflect on Your Vision.

---

1 http://www.businessweek.com/magazine/content/05_40/b3953611.htm
2 http://www.businessweek.com/magazine/content/05_40/b3953611.htm

The human body and mind are fascinating beyond belief. The body has ten major organ systems, while the brain, weighing less than three pounds, has an enormous amount of responsibility. But like any other machine the body and the mind begin to wear out and break down over time. A vacation is a great way to give both the body and mind the well deserved break that they likely need.

World class athletes, who get paid millions of dollars to perform, are fully aware of the importance of rest. Chuck Liddell, one of the most feared men to ever grace the Octagon knows the importance of rest to his success. His workout routine consists of working out one day and resting the next, totaling three days each week when he pushes himself. In UFC (Ultimate Fighting Championship) 79, Liddell's salary was reportedly $500,000.[3] Just think—he rested two out of five days to make that salary. Without rest, your body and mind experience negative effects.

Some of the effects of fatigue include:
- reduced decision-making ability
- reduced ability to do complex planning
- reduced communication skills
- reduced productivity / performance
- reduced attention and vigilance
- reduced ability to handle stress on the job

I think we can all agree that the above list of effects won't lead to positive outcomes in business. Imagine the impact a non-productive or unfocused employee has on a business.

We must also have rest to go about the demands of our daily life…if we want to live successful lives. Without rest, we will not be motivated to try new and exciting things. We may not be motivated or focused enough to deal with important life issues such as managing our budget, or dealing positively with our spouse, our children and our friends.

To effectively achieve a prosperous life, you must factor rest and relaxation into your daily life. The importance of good old R&R

---

3 http://en.wikipedia.org/wiki/UFC_79

should never be taken for granted. Though it's hard to accurately measure the financial impacts of getting enough or not getting enough rest, I would simply say, you owe this to yourself!

Reconnect with Family and Friends

My mother had seven brothers and sisters, all of whom lived in Milwaukee during my childhood years. My dad had one sister who also lived in Milwaukee with her kids. It was common for our family to load the car and take the then six hour voyage to "Brew City." To this day I still have memories of getting off the freeway and going inside my grandmother's house (where it was mandatory that you removed your shoes). We would try to see as many family members as possible while my mother and father caught up with old friends and we reconnected with our cousins.

Before the end of every trip we would end up at my Uncle Dan's and Aunt Henrietta's; this is where the partying began. We would dance, laugh, and play games while the adults shared old stories until late into the night. This is yet another benefit to taking vacations. As a kid I have only fond memories of these getaways, and I recall everyone being happy when we were all together, even if the occasion

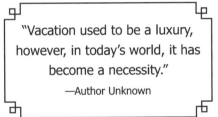

"Vacation used to be a luxury, however, in today's world, it has become a necessity."
—Author Unknown

that brought us together was a sad one. I think we can all agree that laughter is a form of therapy that costs you nothing but pays huge dividends. What's funny is nothing has changed; we still congregate at my aunt and uncle's whenever we are all in town.

These vacations are great for your family and for your business.

Reflect on Your Vision

Being on vacation, in a relaxed and peaceful environment, is a great time to reflect on your vision and mission. Experiencing the

149

stress and pressures of everyday life can be a major contributor to our vision becoming blurred. When you are away from the distractions of life, your mind starts to clear and you are better able to focus.

Creating a vision statement for your life may require you to go on a short vacation. Use some of your vacation time to focus on your vision and mission statements. Create them or tweak them to make sure your actions are in alignment with your goals. During this time you may also want to look at your strategic plan for accomplishing your vision. When vacationing with family, take some time for yourself. You might read a book while the rest of the family is at the pool, take a walk alone, or just meditate in a quiet spot. When you take the time to reflect on your vision, confirm that it is "you" and that you are growing your vision, you will feel the recharging effect that vacations are designed to give.

The Planning Process

Often the reason cited for people not taking a vacation is that they can't afford it. The reality is that you cannot afford not to take a vacation! However, vacations do require financial, geographic and chronological planning. Vacations should be factored in to your annual budget. This is one of the best opportunities for the family to come together and make decisions as a committee. Planning a vacation itself is a form of therapy that can help dissipate anxiety brought on by everyday life. Planning a vacation is another task that takes time, so I recommend starting months in advance with a timeline for completion.

In 2003, I "planned" to take a trip to Africa with two other individuals. The plans were to fly into Nairobi, meet another friend who is native to Kenya, drive to Kenya and spend a week there enjoying the country and hopefully other parts of the continent. We purchased the tickets, obtained passports and the proper immunizations. Together we planned the trip fairly well logistically.

At the time I lived in Las Vegas and had some pressing business matters in Minnesota so I flew from Las Vegas to Minnesota,

150

intending to leave for Africa from the international airport there. I was building a house in Minnesota that was near completion and a family was waiting to close on the property. When I arrived in Minnesota I discovered numerous issues with the project that could not be left unaddressed. One of the other travelers happened to be a partner on the project so one of us had to stay behind to see the project to fruition. That someone ended up being me! My two friends left without me and I never made it to Africa. To this day, I have never been to Africa and don't see it happening in the near future. I blew my opportunity at a dream vacation.

There was a great deal of preparation for this major — and what I considered to be life changing--trip. However, planning involves more than just purchasing the tickets and making other travel arrangements. The old saying "the devil is in the details," is true and I found that out the hard way.

Missing the trip was actually a symptom of a much bigger ailment in my life. The house project had a schedule per se. However, I never focused much on the schedule and I certainly did not plan my trip around the project, making certain to build in time for its completion. The simple fact that I was checking on the project the same day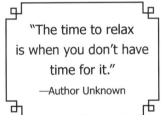

"The time to relax is when you don't have time for it."

—Author Unknown

I was supposed to depart for this once in-in-a-lifetime vacation was a sure sign that the planning process was seriously flawed.

Time

If you have an employer, that employer usually builds paid vacation time into the company benefits package. The typical amount of time allocated is two weeks per year. Fortune 500 Companies prefer their employees to use this time off for an extended vacation rather than a day at a time. They know the extended time away increases an employee's benefits from the vacation. Although many people do not take the full two weeks at one time, I encourage you to take off at least one full week at a time to fully prepare and 'recover' from your time off. Time is an important factor. Determine how much time to set aside for your vacation.

Another aspect of time is getting the "timing" right. In my personal situation, I allocated the time — one week in Africa — but my timing was way off. There were too many other things going on in my life that could, and did, interfere with my vacation plans. You should assess health issues, work projects and personal projects as well as the activities and obligations of other family members when planning your vacation. The entire family should be involved in the planning process to ensure that there are no last minute conflicts. Oftentimes a certain time of the year is best for a family vacation, especially if your children are involved in seasonal sports, camps and other activities.

Budget

Every family should have a vacation fund and create a budget for it. For many, the overall concept of budgeting is new and can seem overwhelming. Budgeting for smaller things like vacations can be a great learning tool for creating and learning the budgeting process. It can also reinforce skills you may have already learned. Vacations are not designed to break the bank; with proper planning, affordable and desirable vacations are within your reach. (The Internet is great for this.)

Decide in advance what sites and activities you will do while vacationing. Knowing what and when you will do activities could have a profound impact on your bottom line, as some activities are cheaper at different times of the year, and some activities may require travel time or other expenses such as taking a cab, bus or subway.

The first step in budgeting is to determine how much you have available to spend on a vacation. Once you determine that figure, plan around it, not over it. The worksheet on the following page will help you to account for most of the possible expenses associated with a vacation.

VACATION PLANNING - BUDGET

Expenses	Budget	Actual	Expenses	Budget	Actual
Transportation			Food & Drink		
Airfare	$	$	Snacks	$	$
Parking at Airport	$	$	Drinks	$	$
Car Rental	$	$	Breakfasts	$	$
Gas	$	$	Lunches	$	$
Tolls	$	$	Dinners	$	$
Bus Tickets	$	$	Groceries	$	$
All-inclusive Vacation	$	$	Bar Tab	$	$
Other:	$	$	Other:	$	$
Insurance			Tickets		
Travel Insurance	$	$	Museums	$	$
Other:	$	$	Amusement Parks	$	$
			Night Club Covers	$	$
Lodging			Shows	$	$
Hotels, Campsite B&B	$	$	Other Expenses	$	$
Other:	$	$	_____	$	$
			_____	$	$
Things to Buy at Home			_____	$	$
Suitcases	$	$	_____	$	$
Clothes	$	$	_____	$	$
Guide Books and					
Reading Material	$	$	_____	$	$
Other:	$	$	_____	$	$
Other:	$	$	_____	$	$
			_____	$	$
To Buy During Vacation			_____	$	$
Souvenirs	$	$	_____	$	$
Clothes	$	$	_____	$	$
Alcohol	$	$	_____	$	$
Other:	$	$	_____	$	$
_____	$	$	_____	$	$
_____	$	$	_____	$	$
_____	$	$	**Summary Calculation**	**Budget**	**Actual**
_____	$	$	Expenses Total	$	$

153

Notice that there is an "Actual" expense column. Fill in this column when you return from vacation to assist in accurately planning for your next vacation.

Location

Where to go for your vacation is a personal preference. However, keep in mind that timing plays a major role in making your decision. Here are a few things to consider:

- How much money did you budget? Vacations further away from home will likely cost more than a closer location.
- How many days will you use for your vacation? When going places with many attractions and activities, you must ensure you are there long enough to see and do all the things you planned to do.
- Will you be vacationing "in season" or "off season?" Vacationing in the off season has its advantages and often allows you to choose a destination that is beyond your budget during peak times of the year.

There are no steadfast rules for deciding where to go on vacation. As long as it fits into your budget, go and have fun.

Staycation

Opting for a "staycation" is a fairly new concept. In 2009 Merriam-Webster added the word staycation to its dictionary. It means a period of time in which an individual or family "stays" and relaxes at home or at a nearby hotel, possibly taking day trips to area attractions.[4]

Taking a staycation has the same mental and psychological effect as taking a traditional vacation. When planned properly, this type of escape can be very affordable and just as rewarding. Staycations usually allow more time to actually relax, can be more budget-friendly, reduce the likelihood of travel mishaps and put fewer miles on the family vehicle; all of which have a positive effect on your bottom line.

---

4 http://en.wikipedia.org/wiki/Staycation

What a Vacation Isn't

I think the best way to demonstrate what a vacation isn't is by starting with the definition of the word.

Definition of VACATION

1: a respite or a time of respite from something: INTERMISSION

2a: a scheduled period during which activity (as of a court or school) is suspended b: a period of exemption from work granted to an employee

3: a period spent away from home or business in travel or recreation <had a restful *vacation* at the beach>

4: an act or an instance of vacating[5]

A few key words stand out: respite, intermission, suspended, and the phrase: away from home or business.

These are all important things to remember. People often treat their vacation like it's an extension of their office—wrong move! You owe it to yourself and your family to make a clean break.

Taking work with you while on vacation is a direct contradiction to the definition of the word and is more of a set back to your business than you think. The work you are doing suffers, the vacation you think you are taking suffers and you return just as drained as when you left.

The other cardinal mistake people make is trying to incorporate a family vacation into a business trip. This type of vacation has very little chance of providing the rest, relaxation and togetherness that you and your family deserve.

The Prosperous Life's Vacation Checklist

Learning how to vacation, like everything else, requires practice. I got very little benefit from taking vacations because I never

---

learned how to take one. I didn't glide in to my vacation, I skidded into my vacation and burned rubber out of my vacations, I would work up until the flight attendant would tell me to turn my phone off and would have meetings scheduled within the hour of my arrival. In one word, insane!

I have just recently learned how to take a vacation, I must say, having changed all my other bad habits has made learning how to vacation simple. In 2009, after watching the Carnival Cruise ship leave without me (yes, I missed the boat), I realized I needed to have a checklist to work from, hence the creation of the below list:

THE PROSPEROUS LIFE'S VACATION CHECKLIST

Home

- Bills to Pay Before Vacation
- Mortgage/Rent
- Utilities
- Car Note
- Insurance
- Cell Phone
- Notify Alarm Company of Plans
- Turn on House Alarm when Leaving
- Mail – Make sure someone picks up mail OR notify Post Office to hold mail
- Secure Valuables
- Turn Lights and Electronics Off
- Check Thermostat
- Double Check Doors and Windows

Trip

Hotel Room Booked: Phone # _____

Confirmation #_____

Air Fare Booked: Flight #_____

Rental Car Booked: Phone #_____

Confirmation #_____

Miscellaneous

- Refill Prescriptions
- Get Cash/Check Credit Card Balances
- Family members and an emergency contact have a copy of the itinerary

Automobile

- Tune Up
- Check Tires, Battery, Fluids
- Get Maps
- Ensure that car insurance is up to date
- Fill gas tank

THE PROSPEROUS LIFE'S VACATION TO-DO LIST

I would like to add this personal checklist of things to do while on vacation:

- Continue to work out
- Eat great tasting meals with sensible portions
- Plan time to be lazy (rest)
- Sleep well
- Take long showers or baths
- Do something you have never done before
- Take a lot of pictures

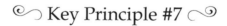 Key Principle #7

Vacations

Plan and take vacations with your family.

Every successful business person knows the importance of breaking away from day-to-day routines. You and your family owe this to one another.

Chapter 8

Key Principle #8

Marriage

Marriage

=

Merger

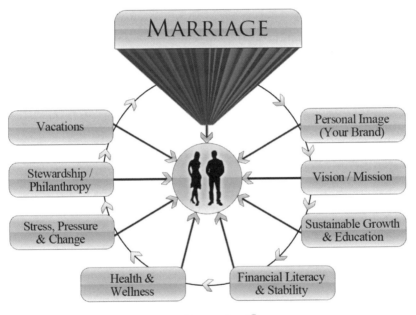

The Life Is A Business! ™
Blueprint To Prosperity

"Love is blind – marriage is the eye-opener."

—Pauline Thomason

Delta

Delta CEO:	Richard H. Anderson
Number of Employees:	81,106
Fortune 500 Ranking:	#84
Industry:	Airlines
Location:	Atlanta, GA
Annual Revenue:	$28.0B

Just as a delta is a symbol for change in math, Delta Air Lines symbolizes the changing mathematics of the airline industry. Delta became the world's largest airline, based on traffic statistics, after its $2.8 billion merger with Northwest Airlines in 2008. Through its regional carriers (including subsidiary Comair), the combined company serves more than 365 destinations in more than 65 countries, and it operates a mainline fleet of about 800 aircraft. Delta is a founding member of the SkyTeam marketing and code-sharing alliance (allowing airlines to sell tickets on one another's flights and thus extend their networks), which includes carriers such as Air France and KLM.[1]

---

1 www.hoovers.com

❧ Growing Your Enterprise ❧

"Will you marry me?"

"Yes!" she screams.

Love is in the air and all is right with the world.

The engagement period is joyful. The wedding is planned down to the tiniest detail and will be forever memorable. The honeymoon brings you closer together. Then, your life as a married couple begins and—seemingly out of nowhere—you find yourself in disagreement about a vast array of topics, both big and small: finances, children, whose family to spend the holidays with, who is responsible for which household chores, and whether or not that lime green, corduroy rocker/recliner with the well-worn armrests and annoying squeak gets to stay or go. To one it is a treasure; to the other it is an eyesore. Suddenly, you are both wondering if joining your two separate lives into one was the right decision.

When you decide to marry, you are deciding to grow your "enterprise." You each bring an individual set of routines, habits, expectations, and values that must now be integrated to create a mutually satisfying and functioning new set of routines, habits, expectations, and values.

This union is much like a corporate merger, bringing with it a similar structure with similar challenges.

Comparison: Merger—Marriage	
Fortune 500 Company: Merger	**Your Prosperous Life: Marriage**
Two companies see a brighter future together than apart and decide to merge.	Two individuals fall in love, see a brighter future together than apart and decide to marry.
A legal and binding contract is signed.	A legal and binding contract is signed.
Decisions about the future of the company are discussed and agreed to.	Decisions about becoming a family and the future are discussed and agreed to.

161

There are company officers and stakeholders who are directly affected by corporate decisions.	All family members have a role to play and a "stake" in the decisions that are made.
Company officers oversee day-to-day operations, handle the finances, direct employees to stay focused on the corporate vision and mission, and protect the company's reputation.	Spouses oversee day-to-day household matters, handle the finances, raise the children, stay focused on mutual beliefs and values and establish expectations to build the family's reputation.
Officers of a successful merger: trust each other, are competent, have good communication skills, are willing and able to work together, and make adjustments when needed.	Individuals in a successful marriage: trust each other, are competent, have good communication skills, are willing and able to work together, and make adjustments when needed.

Marriage is a Merger, Not an Acquisition

A merger is the combination of entities from two to one. An acquisition is the act of gaining (acquiring) a possession.

In business, acquisitions are complicated to execute but the result is clear: one company buys another. The buying company makes the rules and the acquired company lives by them. Simple. In a merger, two companies agree to combine their strengths, workforce, and resources. A new company emerges designed to be stronger together than they were individually. Not so simple.

This chapter's case study, the Delta-Northwest merger, created the largest airline in the world. It took months of talks to first determine if it was right for both individual airlines. I'm certain that the vision and mission for each airline was carefully studied. I'm certain they compared purchasing habits, bookkeeping practices, policies and procedures, social responsibility agendas, credit ratings, company net worth, and the overall reputation of the companies and their corporate leaders.

Once the determination was made by both parties that they could merge (marry) and grow stronger, it then took many more months of strategizing to seamlessly make the merger happen. The success of the Delta-Northwest merger is a tribute to the understanding and process of objective assessment and ultimate commitment.

In contrast, the Time Warner and AOL merger in 2001 and its subsequent separation in 2009 marked the biggest corporate merger failure of modern times. It was described by CNBC's anchor and reporter David Faber as the "marriage from hell."[1] The failure of this much-celebrated media marriage can be attributed to a multitude of things but, in the end, the breakdown occurred due to insufficient research, poor planning, and lack of communication. These are essential to the success of every corporate merger.

These same practices apply to a marriage. Getting married is the merging of two previously individual brands. Some brands work well together, and others, not so well. Unfortunately, because marriage is a decision primarily based on emotion, people fail to do the preliminary work required to ensure that it is a good, strong, and sustaining decision.

Individuals headed down the aisle will say they are entering into a merger. However, most act like it is an acquisition. The expectation is that little will change. The reality is that, to be successful, a lot must change to accommodate both individuals' needs and wants while building a future together. What's "yours" and what's "mine" will now become "ours."

In my opinion, the decision to get married is the biggest business decision you will ever make in your life of prosperity.

The first time I traveled with the woman who is now my wife, was in November of 1996. We flew together to Las Vegas to witness the first fight between Mike Tyson and Evander Holyfield. After the fight, our plan was to drive from Las Vegas to Los Angeles to visit her family. I intended to drive but Las Vegas had gotten the best of me the night before so we agreed she would take the first leg of driving duties. We hit the road and I immediately fell asleep. Midway through the trip I awoke to discover her speeding on the open road in the California desert. I won't say how fast she was driving, but I will say she was hauling butt! She was fearless. She was confident. She was (pardon the pun) driven.

I knew right then and there that this was the woman I would marry.

---

1 http://www.cnbc.com/id/34448278/

164

STOP RIGHT HERE!

Who makes a lifelong decision based on miles per hour?

Me.

Who, after a weekend trip to Vegas, thought that was enough time to decide on a lifelong partner?

Me.

I was in love and I decided that I must share my life with this person.

In marriage, potential partners usually lead with their hearts. In a corporate merger, potential partners lead with their heads. Yet, the truth is that there are just as many failed mergers—both in business and in life—as there are successes.

I was lucky. Despite making an irresponsible and irrational assessment of the type of person who would make a good mate, and struggling through some very difficult times, our marriage has survived. Yet, if we knew then what we know now about preparing for our merger, the ground beneath us would not have been so shaky and the struggles would not have been so hard.

The prosperous life requires a merger that is more than love and more than a naïve perspective that "happily ever after" is the natural course of marriage. It isn't. If you want a happily-ever-after life, you must plan for it.

You must discuss the "tough stuff" even if it feels intrusive or uncomfortable. Find out where each of you stands on topics like: how many, if any, kids does each want, religion, where to live (headquarters), credit ratings and education plans. These are just a few of the hundreds of questions that should be asked and answered between the two of you. If one or both of you says the words, "it's none of your business," then that's a clear warning sign that you are not ready to merge your lives together.

Far too often, out of fear of conflict, we avoid asking the tough questions, we fail to delve deep and, ultimately, marriages that could have survived, fail. A 2008 statistic estimated that 40 to 50 percent of all marriages end in divorce. On average, first marriages that end in divorce last about eight years.[2] This trend is a leading factor in why

---

2 www.wikipedia.org

our prosperous lives never see their full potential. Companies ask the tough questions day in and day out, and so should you.

Preparation: Pre-marriage Planning

Divorce can create the type of devastation from which many never fully recover. Heightened trust issues and feelings of failure chip away at self esteem and children in particular can suffer irreparable damage from such a catastrophic event. That's why proper vetting is required for your life of prosperity before entering into your marital merger.

In many cultures, arranged marriages are viewed as a social and economic necessity, the terms of which are agreed upon by the families of the future groom and bride. Whether or not the bride and groom are in love is not a priority; what's important is that the marriage is stable with staying power.[3] Cultures that favor arranged marriages view marriage as a business. While I am not advocating for arranged marriages, I would contend that the process is worth examining. A planned life union is more likely to succeed than one that is not planned. Compatibility becomes more important than the "chemistry" of attraction. Factors considered in the matchmaking process include: Reputation, Vocation, Wealth, Religion, Diet and Age.[4]

> "After you marry, every asset either of you acquires is jointly held. That's why you both need to be in sync on your long-term financial goals, from paying off the mortgage to putting away for retirement. Ideally, you should talk about all this before you wed. If you don't, you can end up deeply frustrated and financially spent."
>
> —Suze Orman

You can have the best of both worlds—attraction and compatibility. Attraction is natural and organic. Compatibility requires exploration and questioning. Below is a list of things to consider prior to getting married:

---

3 www.professorshouse.com
4 www.wikipedia.org

- Do you have the same or similar long term vision?
- Do you share the same or similar values; honesty, integrity, loyalty?
Do either of you have looming legal matters; pending lawsuits, child support, liens or judgments, prior criminal history?
- Do you know and support each other's individual goals and aspirations?
- Are you on the same plane spiritually?
- Do you want to have children? If so, how many and what are your philosophies for child rearing, discipline, and stay-at-home parenting?
- What is each others' financial situation and how do you handle money?
- Do you have differences in priorities and expectations of your life together?

The more you learn about each other as potential partners, the greater your chances for a successful marriage. Who wouldn't want that?

Examination: Top Deal Breakers

In the above list of considerations, two factors top the list of causes for divorce in the United States: finances and differences in priorities and expectations. Let's examine these two top offenders more closely.

Deal-breaking Culprit #1: Finances

Arguments about money—how to save it, how to spend it, who can spend it, how much you can spend without first discussing it with your spouse, and whether or not you each can have "your own" money to do with whatever you please—will strain your marriage. Not just a little—a lot! It's probably the most important discussion you should have before marriage, yet time and time again, couples don't bother talking about the details of handling money. This results in misunderstandings and disagreements about financial affairs and drives a wedge between partners.

When the conflict is not resolved, the wedge is driven further into the fabric of the relationship and often severs the partnership.

The ideal time to deal with money matters is in the pre-marital planning stages.

No two people share the exact same philosophy about how to handle money—that's okay. Yet, an in-depth discussion about finances is critical to lay the groundwork for money management once you join lives and households. Be honest with your partner, and be open to ideas for new ways to do things. Remember that you share a mutual goal and you are both responsible to work out an arrangement that will ensure you achieve it.

Before merging finances, talk about what each of you does individually, what your financial goals are together, and how you're going to reach them. Some of the topics to discuss include:

- Spending habits.
- Who will be the CFO (Chief Financial Officer), overseeing day-to-day financial activities, balancing the checkbook, and tracking 'what goes where' for income and output.
- The amount of debt you each have, what the plan is for reducing current debt, and how you will avoid creating more debt.
- Setting up bank accounts: decide if you will pool all of your money into one joint account, maintain individual accounts, or have a "yours, mine, and ours" setup with three separate accounts.

Deal-breaking Culprit #2: Differences in Priorities and Expectations

Conflict usually results from differences in priorities and expectations when two businesses or two people join together to become one entity. Conflict is a concept innate to marriage since you are attempting to join two sets of fully formed opinions, habits, and philosophies. Fortunately, this can be managed effectively with proper planning.

168

Plans for conflict resolution exist in all Fortune 500 Companies and one should be in place for you and your family. You have to be able to disagree without being disagreeable. It is important to question or criticize the behavior or action, not the person. Actually, having conflict and learning to resolve it can strengthen family bonds. When we learn how to express how we feel, speak clearly to one another, and truly listen to each other, we are exercising our "emotional muscle," and growing into a maturity that makes the business stronger.

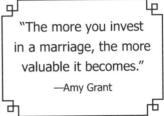

"The more you invest in a marriage, the more valuable it becomes."
—Amy Grant

This type of growth—or lack of it—can be passed down through generations when children witness our behavior. Always be mindful of what you are saying and how you are saying it, especially when your children are watching. Conflict resolution is a skill that will serve you well in all of your relationships.

Commitment: Communication and Role Identification

When we consider the fundamentals of mergers and marriages, commitment is at the very core.

Officers of corporations sign on the dotted line and seal the deal with a handshake. Couples sign on the dotted line and seal the deal with words like, "For richer and for poorer, in sickness and in health...all the days of our lives..." You make promises to be together through the good times and the bad.

Fulfilling a commitment, whether it is a Fortune 500 Company or your life of prosperity, requires you to focus on two key components:

1) the ability to clearly express and discuss your thoughts, ideas, and concerns with your partner (communication), and

2) identification of who is responsible for what tasks/chores to be completed (roles/job titles).

There's a saying, "there's nothing like an understanding." It's very simple and very true, but the only way to reach an understanding is through communication. By sharing insights and opinions and discussing how best to move forward, we can get ahead of conflict and put ourselves in a position to act rather than react.

> "Marriage is like a business investment. Its long term viability is best established unemotionally."
> —Author Unknown

In marriages, the importance of developing great communication skills can't be stressed enough. Husbands and wives need to be great communicators with each other as well as with their children. The practice of sitting down as a family and having meaningful verbal exchanges to create understanding is a business decision far too few families commit to doing.

We live in an age where we have finger-tip access to information that is transferred in record speed. Unfortunately, amid the electronic communications peppered with abbreviations and emoticons, a lot is lost in translation. Misunderstandings occur and escalate into conflict.

Families must have a clear agreement on how important information is exchanged. Use technology if it enhances the process, but never omit face-to-face gatherings where you can close yourselves off from outside distractions and focus on genuine, look-me-in-the-eye conversation and discussion.

> TIP: Communication requires an exchange of information, not a filibuster. The key to effective communication is the ability to listen. You will never learn anything if you are the only one talking.

Family Matters: Defining Roles in Your Life of Prosperity

Corporate executives have defined roles and responsibilities and so should your family.

Roles & Job Responsibilities	
Fortune 500 Company	**Your Prosperous Life**
CEO (Chief Executive Officer) The CEO is responsible for communicating the vision of the company to both internal and external audiences. The CEO lays the groundwork for the company's strategy to accomplish goals, including economic well being.	CEO (Chief Executive Officer) The Prosperous Life CEO is responsible for communicating the family vision and mission to internal and external audiences. The CEO lays the groundwork for the family's strategy to accomplish goals, including economic well being.
CFO (Chief Financial Officer) One of the CFO's primary responsibilities is to bring financial controls to a company. Controls include the management of cash flow and overhead expenses. The CFO also tracks expenditures and balances the budget.	CFO (Chief Financial Officer) The Prosperous Life CFO keeps close track of all money matters from the basics of paying the bills and balancing the checkbook to monitoring accounts, tracking expenditures, and assessing the financial health of the family.
COO (Chief Operations Officer) The COO is responsible for processes and procedures that keep day-to-day operations running smoothly. The COO keeps the organization energized and is often the person who pays attention to the details while the CEO pays attention to the bigger picture.	COO (Chief Operations Officer) The Prosperous Life COO maintains a tactical, hands-on involvement in day-to-day activities for the family and determines and enforces the procedures for maintaining the household. The COO pays attention to the details while the CEO pays attention to the bigger picture.
Stakeholders In corporations, internal stakeholders are those who are directly engaged in economic transactions, like stockholders, suppliers, creditors, customers, and employees. External stakeholders are those who can be affected or can affect a company's actions, like activist groups, communities and government.	Stakeholders In your Prosperous Life, the primary stakeholders are you, your spouse, and your children. They are directly affected by, or can affect, every decision you make or action you take. Secondary stakeholders include teachers, community groups, and extended family members such as grandparents.

171

As in every good merger, roles and responsibilities must be defined so everyone is clear about "who does what" in the organization. Likewise, your life of prosperity needs clearly identified roles and responsibilities for each family member. When you are single, you are responsible for everything. However, when you marry, identify who will be responsible for what tasks—this helps to avoid duplication of efforts.

Unlike corporations, you can be more flexible with responsibility assignment. For example, one person may not be great at all aspects of the CFO's job. You may decide that one spouse will pay the bills and balance the checkbook, and the other will assess how well the family is meeting its long-term financial goals. Similarly, the COO may identify "procedures" and create a schedule or chart for tasks to be performed, but other family members are assigned duties to be carried out, like trash removal, clearing dishes from the table after meals, and folding laundry.

The goal is to know what your combined responsibilities are and identify who will become accountable for each one.

Children as Stakeholders

I briefly identified stakeholders in the Roles and Job Responsibiities chart, but let's take a closer look at how children are part of the prosperous life.

Stakeholders in a Fortune 500 Company consist of the shareholders, employees, consumer and the community at large. In the business setting, the most important stakeholders are the shareholders who have invested money into the company and are expecting a return.

In your marriage, your children are your stakeholders. Many couples think of children as a byproduct of the union—important to us because we love them. But every decision that you make and every action that you take impacts your children's lives directly, and children often have their own opinions of how the family unit could function better. That makes them stakeholders in your life of prosperity.

Internal Stakeholders — External Stakeholders

Spouse / Significant Other, Children, Immediate Family — Your Fortune 500 Life — Society, Creditors, Government, Employer

The lack of planning prior to marriage and during the marriage can greatly impact our children's lives. Children rely on the adults in their lives, usually parents, for each and every aspect of their development including:

- Shelter
- Health and wellness
- Education
- Physical development
- Mental and emotional development
- Financial literacy
- Spirituality

I recall a conversation I once had with my wife regarding our daughter. My wife asked if I felt obligated to pay for her to attend college. I replied, "No." However, I then began to give it more serious thought. If I insist that she attend college, perhaps I should be willing to participate in paying for it. My wife went on to tell me that she expected to help our daughter buy her first house once she graduated from college as a way to help jump-start her life.

I never knew my wife's plan for our daughter, which was very different from my admittedly sketchy plan to let our child make her own way in life. We had failed to discuss our desires and intentions for our daughter.

When two people marry/merge, their decisions will set the tone for the development of their current and/or future children's lives. Each partner brings a different life experience and, now that they are one entity, decisions must be made for the child that will guide their self-development of health and wellness, financial ability and spirituality. Proper grounding in these areas begins with parents deciding how they will present these issues to the children.

For example, if one parent is vegan and the other loves eating steak, they must have a conversation and make decisions about food and food choices as it will impact the stakeholders — the children.

Perhaps even more important, if the parents have completely opposite views on saving and financial literacy, the children may not be able to grasp an understanding of how to handle money. The child is exposed to both a financially sound role model and a financially frivolous role model. This can impact the stakeholder in two ways.

First, the child develops mixed financial literacy skills and struggles to balance the two extremes. Second, the financial

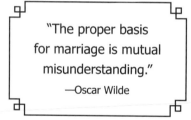

"The proper basis for marriage is mutual misunderstanding."
—Oscar Wilde

illiteracy of the frivolous spender can negatively impact the overall finances of the family and cause a trickle-down effect that limits the activities and educational opportunities for the child. This creates stress in the marriage, which directly impacts the emotional development of the child and the overall functioning of the family. This is evidence of a "blurred" vision as discussed in Key Principle #1.

The bottom line is that couples must realize that children are stakeholders in the family unit. It is one thing to make allowances for and overlook differences in each other "in the name of love" when there is just the two of you. It is quite another thing to allow those differences to remain unresolved once you have children.

Have a candid discussion about the potential implications that your individual habits and philosophies will have on the family as a whole.

Already Married? Don't Panic!

If you are currently married and never engaged in pre-marital planning, it is not too late! One of the advantages for you is that you now know what you should have known then.

Return to Key Principle #1, but this time with your spouse. This will allow both of you to share your vision for your life as individuals and then work on a vision for your family. Once that vision is in place, individually prepare a list of issues that you think have caused problems in your marriage. Be honest about each issue. Once you have prepared this list, celebrate. You have accomplished more than the average married couple in the United States.

Come back together and review each other's list. The list will have some common items, some opposing items, and some that may surprise you. Spend time together developing a workable strategy that will get you through these issues. Be sure to incorporate lessons learned in Key Principle #3, and remember to employ your conflict resolution skills as discussed in the Communication section of this chapter.

Marriage Does Not Necessarily End at Divorce or Even Death

In Key Principle #5 we discussed briefly the marriage and divorce of Anna Nicole Smith and Howard Marshall in connection with risk and crisis management. The emphasis was on proper planning in life and in anticipation of death to avoid crisis and to effectively manage risk. I emphasized the fact that the decisions we make can supersede our death.

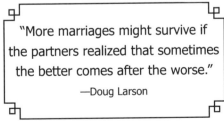

"More marriages might survive if the partners realized that sometimes the better comes after the worse."
—Doug Larson

As stated earlier in this chapter, marriage is truly a merger between two "businesses." That decision to merge can have an impact beyond both death and divorce. Once connected, many things continue to bind you together after death and/or divorce. Social Security benefits are a prime example of that long-term connectedness. This is a large area of law so I will focus on Social Security and divorced women to make my point.

If you are a divorced woman, you can receive benefits based on your ex-husband's work if:

- Your marriage lasted ten years or longer,

- You are unmarried

- You are age 62 or older

- The benefit you are entitled to receive based on your own work is less than the benefits you would receive on your husband's work; and

- Your ex-husband is entitled to Social Security retirement or disability benefits.

If your husband is deceased, you can receive benefits:
- At age 60, or age 50 if you are disabled, if your marriage lasted at least ten years, and you are not entitled to a higher benefit on your own record.

- At any age if you are caring for his child who also is your natural or legally adopted child and younger than 16 or disabled and entitled to benefits. Your benefits will continue until the child reaches age 16 or is no longer disabled. You can receive this benefit even though you were not married to your ex-husband for ten years.

This is a prime example of how a woman, now divorced, can benefit from her prior marriage. It can make a huge difference in the quality of life of a woman who may not have earned sufficient income during her working years to live a quality retirement. This is an example of a business decision that has a continual financial impact.

❧ Key Principle #8 ❧

Marriage

Enter marriage with the same caution and consideration as you would a business merger.

Marriage is one of the biggest life decisions you will ever make – treat it with the respect it deserves to set yourself up for success.

Chapter 9

Key Principle #9

Personal Image (Reputation)

Personal Image (Reputation)

=

Corporate Brand

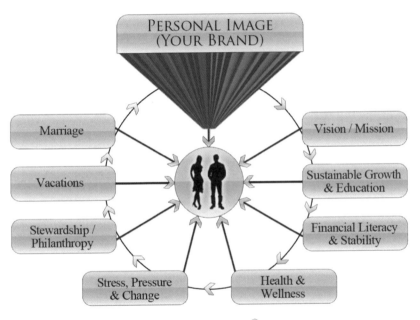

The Life Is A Business! ™
Blueprint To Prosperity

"It takes 20 years to build a reputation and five minutes to ruin it. If you think about that, you'll do things differently."
—Warren Buffett, investor, industrialist, philanthropist

Case Study

UPS

UPS CEO:	Scott Davis
Number of Employees:	408,000
Fortune 500 Ranking:	#43
Industry:	Shipping
Location:	Atlanta, GA
Annual Revenue:	$45.3B

Headquartered in Atlanta, Georgia, United Parcel Service (UPS) is the world's largest package delivery company, transporting some 15 million packages and documents per business day throughout the U.S. and to more than 200 countries and territories. Its delivery operations use a fleet of about 100,000 motor vehicles and about 500 aircraft. In addition to package delivery, the company offers services such as logistics and freight forwarding through UPS Supply Chain Solutions, and less-than-truckload (LTL) freight transportation through UPS Ground Freight. (LTL carriers combine freight from multiple shippers into a single truckload.)[1]

---

1 www.hoovers.com

You Are Known By the Company You Keep

UPS has a distinctive brand that aligns with its corporate beliefs. The company spends time and money to ensure that its brand is well known and that company relationships and employee actions solidify its reputation to its many audiences. Each of us also has a brand.

For a long time, I was doing things that didn't align with my beliefs. I was going places where I shouldn't have been going. I was spending time with people whose values were in direct opposition to mine in both business and their personal lives. I began emulating behaviors that were counterproductive, and I lost track of my vision — actually, I hadn't fully developed my vision. Because of my haphazard actions, my reputation — my 'brand' — paid the price. And it has taken me a considerable amount of time to rebuild it.

For a life of prosperity, our brand — our reputation — is what we as individuals or as a family want to project to the world. Reputations, good or bad, are built on our actions and our associations — what we do, the places we spend our time, and who we spend our time with.

Essentially, for both Fortune 500 Companies and your prosperous life, you are known by the company you keep.

Corporate Branding

So what is a brand? A brand is the "identity of a specific product, service, or business. A brand can take many forms, including a name, sign, symbol, or slogan. The word brand began simply as a way to tell one person's cattle from another by means of a hot iron stamp and has continued to evolve to encompass identity - in effect the personality of a product, company or service."[1]

---

1 www.wikipedia.com

For the purpose of this book, I want to focus on corporate branding rather than product branding because the corporate brand is about relationships — what a company wants to be known for and project to the world — in short, its reputation.

A corporate brand is crucial to the identity of the company. The purpose of corporate branding is to increase the awareness of the products or services behind the brand and to set certain expectations that promote the brand's quality and characteristics as well as the company's vision and mission.

For corporations, the benefits of branding include things like: customer loyalty, differentiation from its competitors, and the perception of authenticity. A strong brand also holds increased market value and can serve as financial leverage if the company is sold, acquired, or merged with another.

A company's brand is typically manifested by the creation of a logo at the company's inception. This iconic symbol is carefully crafted and never easily decided on. This logo, though sometimes redefined over the years, becomes synonymous with the business throughout the life of the business. The logo helps establish and project the company brand and reputation. This reputation is sacred to the company owners and CEO. Some logos are simply the company's name designed in a specific way, like Nike. Other logos are independent symbols like Apple's iconic apple. And, as in our case study, logos can also be stylized acronyms: UPS.

UPS is one of the largest corporate package delivery companies in the world and has one of the most widely recognizable logos. Yet, the logo is just a symbol of

"As you grow, your associates will change. Some of your friends will not want you to go on. They will want you to stay where they are. Friends that don't help you climb will want you to crawl. Your friends will stretch your vision or choke your dream."
—Author Unknown

the brand. Companies must live up to what that logo represents. UPS takes branding seriously, right down to the details. From the familiar big brown trucks (which are washed daily), to the neatly dressed and courteous drivers, to the customer-focused delivery system, UPS has processes and procedures in place to protect its brand in a fiercely competitive marketplace.

Personal Branding

Jay-Z is arguably one of the greatest hip hop MC's of all time. He is one of the most financially successful hip hop artists and entrepreneurs in America having had a net worth of over $450 million in 2010. He has sold approximately 50 million albums worldwide, while receiving ten Grammy Awards for his musical work, and numerous additional nominations. Jay-Z co-owns the 40/40 Club, is part-owner of the NBA's New Jersey Nets and the creator of the Rocawear clothing line. He is the former CEO of Def Jam Recordings, one of the three founders of Roc-A-Fella Records, and the founder of Roc Nation.[2] And to top all of that off, he is married to Beyonce Knowles.

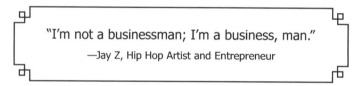

"I'm not a businessman; I'm a business, man."
—Jay Z, Hip Hop Artist and Entrepreneur

The above Jay Z quote is from "Diamonds from Sierra Leone Remix," the "Late Registration" album. Of the best Jay Z quotes, this one tells us just what makes Jay Z himself: he's a business. Just by being who he is, Jay Z rakes in millions, just like business, man.[3]

The Beyonce brand is also worth mentioning. In her own right, Beyonce is a multi-platinum selling artist turned actress who has a clothing line and her own perfume. Knowles, along with band mate Kelly Rowland, founded the Survivor Foundation, a charitable entity set up to provide transitional housing for 2005 Hurricane Katrina victims and storm evacuees in the Houston, Texas area, showcasing her commitment to charitable giving. She refuses to

2 http://en.wikipedia.org/wiki/Jay-Z
3 http://www.mademan..com/mm/10-best-jay-z-quotes.html

talk publicly about her marriage and has never had so much as a near brush with public scandal. She realizes how powerful her individual brand is as well as her marital brand.

Do you wonder how a man could rise from poverty to such great success? By protecting his brand/reputation! Jay-Z is known as a man who means what he says and says what he means. He understands the impact of those he is aligned with, evidenced by the woman he married. As a result, he has gained the respect as a very accomplished businessman.

> "It's not enough to be in the right place at the right time. You have to be the right person in the right place at the right time."
>
> —T. Harv Eker, Secrets of the Millionaire Mind

Just as corporate branding is all about business identity, personal branding is all about your identity. Developing your brand – your image and reputation – and guarding it is a business decision that must be taken seriously. A good reputation will help advance your mission.

Strong corporate branding requires a high level of personal attention and commitment from the CEO and upper management to become fully effective and meet the goals and objectives of the corporation. As the CEO of your prosperous life, you, too, must give it a high level of personal attention and commitment.

Whether you realize it or not, you already have a brand. You might be "that guy who hangs out at the corner bar with his buddies every day after work," or you might be "that guy who takes his kids to the park every day after work." Based on what you do, where you go, who you're with, what you wear, the way you wear it, and even the way you wear your hair, you are 'telling' people something about yourself, your values, and your morals. You are supporting, positively or negatively, your brand.

As much as none of us likes to be judged, the truth is we all do it. All we know of each other is what we observe. You judge others by their behaviors and actions, and others judge you for the same.

Remember:

You are what you believe.

You are who you surround yourself with.

You are what you do.

To believe you can often be seen with a certain group and not be considered a member of that group is naïve. In other words, it's difficult for others to discern you from that group. Don't put them or yourself in that predicament.

Personal branding is very similar to corporate branding:

Corporate Branding versus Personal Branding	
Fortune 500 Corporate Branding	**Prosperous Life Personal Branding**
Requires personal attention and commitment from CEO and management.	Requires personal attention and commitment from you and your family.
Is the manifestation of the corporate vision and mission.	Is the manifestation of your personal vision and mission.
"Tells" its customers, shareholders, vendors, competitors, community, and employees what the company stands for.	"Tells" friends, family, community, employers, coworkers, and anyone in your personal network what you stand for.
Must be maintained and protected.	Must be maintained and protected.

"The Prosperous Life" Steps to Developing your Personal Brand

Developing your brand is a process. I have devised five criteria for developing your personal brand and using that brand to effectively support your life of prosperity:

1. *Know your Vision and Mission:*

To begin creating your personal brand, you must establish a vision and mission. You must know where you want to go in life; who you want to be. Your vision will frame your personal brand. Review Key Principle #1 and the vision and mission statements

186

you prepared for your life. Internalize these statements as the first step in developing your personal brand. Ask yourself, "What do I want to be known for?" Then, position yourself to be that person. That person should be reflected in your actions; what you say and what you do, everyday of your life.

"You are what you believe." The brand a person is selling to the public often contradicts the actions the public sees. In other words, people talk the talk but don't walk the walk. This is why both your vision and your brand must be authentic; they must reflect who you are with 100% accuracy. You must believe in the messages you are conveying. There's nothing worse for your business than being considered a "phony" or "fraud." This is the "poison pill" of your business.

I say again, *you must have a vision for your life* to begin to develop the brand that you want to be known for by other people. More importantly, you must believe in your vision and mission; believe that you have the ability to create the brand that you desire for yourself.

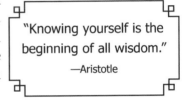

"Knowing yourself is the beginning of all wisdom."
—Aristotle

Your brand must be organic, original, and designed for you and by you. Your brand is one of the few things in this world that is yours and yours alone. Displaying your brand to the world should make you proud! **You must take positive action toward creating your brand.** This is a fundamental step in developing your personal brand, and arguably the most important step. Your vision and mission are the foundation for creating and maintaining your personal brand. It's time to follow your intention with action. The world is eager to see you flourish. Like a Superbowl quarterback, fans want to watch you run the play that you called in the huddle after you hollered "break."

2. *Assess Your Strengths and Weaknesses:*

You must align your reputation to support your vision and mission by assessing your current strengths and weaknesses. Some of us are quick to identify our strengths and struggle to admit our weaknesses. Others of us identify our weaknesses and are hesitant to boast about our strengths. To successfully move forward with your vision and mission, you must do both objectively and honestly.

All humans have limitations beyond our physical strength. Time is very limiting. Over committing can be devastating to your reputation. I personally earned quite a reputation for this. At one point I owned or co-owned four businesses. Each business was labor intensive. Things were so bad at one point that people were waiting in line to talk to me about very important decisions that had to be made. When you over-book yourself the way I did, your attention to detail is fleeting. I once over-paid a sub-contractor by $1,000; sadly, that was the last I saw of him. Time isn't the only thing that may limit us. Oftentimes we simply lack the skill set needed to follow through. Vow never to get caught in this trap but if you do, don't be afraid to let others know you are in over your head. You can maintain, and even gain, respect from others when you are honest about your shortcomings.

> "Your personal brand is a promise to your clients... a promise of quality, consistency, competency, and reliability."
>
> —Jason Hartman

Obviously, you should always play to your strengths. I'm a towering 5'7", so when I played basketball I knew I wasn't going to dunk the ball on a fast break, and I knew I wouldn't be expected to bang in the paint. But I did turn my lack of height into my strength. I was good at getting steals and moving the ball down the floor quickly so I used that strength to my advantage. At every opportunity, accentuate your strengths.

Take the time to make a list of your strengths and weaknesses. Be honest. If there are things that you would like to change, then do so. Strengthen your weaknesses by first acknowledging what they are then finding ways to change what you can or make life adjustments for the things you cannot change.

For example, if it is your vision and mission to spend much of your life educating women in the areas of self esteem, empowerment and self sufficiency, you will need to analyze how your reputation might support that vision and mission and how you will resolve inconsistencies. Your brand and your vision/mission will directly influence each other. If you are a shy person who does not like to speak in front of people, yet your vision is to inspire, your shyness is a weakness you must overcome for the type of vision you detailed. You will have to work toward developing your brand as an eloquent speaker by taking classes, joining Toastmasters, or getting a coach.

It is equally important to assess your strengths. Perhaps you can write persuasive and inspiring content — this will be a huge asset when you are preparing your presentations. You also may be able to reach and empower women through written communications such as books or other training material.

You must also learn to accept what you cannot change…know your limitations. MC Hammer had a vision to be generous. His brand, so to speak, was to be one of generosity, community and compassion. He sought to support that brand by being generous with the money he earned as an entertainer. He gave monetary gifts and support, and added a large number of family and friends to his business' payroll. But he failed to acknowledge that he simply couldn't sustain the million-dollar-a-month payroll he sometimes faced. Despite amassing significant wealth, he had limitations, too.

Good things happen to good people, and though I don't know him personally, when I last saw him being interviewed he appeared to be a happy man again. I'm sure he realigned his vision, and brought his brand more in line with both his vision/mission and his personal ability.

3. *Choose Your Friends Carefully:*

The best way to ruin your reputation is by being associated with people and groups who have a bad reputation or don't align with your vision. This is an easy trap to fall into, especially with family members or a friend you've had since elementary school.

People change, and not always for the better. But you can't allow the reputation of others tarnish your brand. This can also

189

be a problem in a professional/work setting. Spending time with or around a known rebel rouser will give others the impression that this behavior is, or will become, your behavior. Protect and strengthen your brand by associating with people and groups with stellar reputations. It's difficult for the public to separate you from the company you keep. If you are in the company of "bad," they will brand you as bad. This message is important to pass on to your children (shareholders) as well. The people around you and the networks you participate in will either enhance or damage your business/reputation. You have control over which one it will be.

Changing the company that you keep is easier than you think. It can be as simple as joining a list serve for people with similar interests or joining a book club. Both of these small steps allow you to meet new people and align yourself with individuals who support your brand.

4. *Maintain Your Brand:*

Once you have created your personal brand, you must maintain it. Consider the impact that every life decision you make will have on your reputation. For example, if your personal brand includes being a person of great moral character and an advocate for the preservation of the earth and all things natural, being overheard representing a point of view contrary to your brand can destroy the effectiveness of your brand. Therefore, you must consistently and constantly be on guard and avoid engaging in activities that damage the personal brand you have created. You must also revisit and refresh your brand by checking it periodically to insure that it is in line with your vision.

Your brand represents you in the purest form and this must be guarded. It is sacred, which seems like a strong word, but your reputation is serious "business." It is both a snapshot and an x-ray that tells the world who and what you represent. If you agree that nearly every decision we make in life is a business decision (a decision that impacts your bottom line) then you know the importance of reputation.

Golfing great Tiger Woods is a perfect example of someone who understood personal branding. He is also an example of a person who failed to maintain his personal branding. Woods spent a great deal of energy developing his brand. His image reflected a clean cut "All American" guy. He was considered a stellar athlete, a caring community member and a loving family man. Everyone identified with this brand. You may not know him personally, yet would likely describe him using this branded image. For all of Tiger Woods' faults, I give him credit for recognizing, at a young age, that he was a brand.

His downfall in 2009, punctuated by his admission of multiple indiscretions, personifies what happens in the business world when a carefully crafted reputation is disrespected, taken for granted and left unguarded. While a bad reputation can be repaired, it puts a strain on business and finances, and it places a strain on life that may never fully recover from the consequences. Your reputation aligns with your vision.

> "Associate yourself with people of good quality, for it is better to be alone than in bad company."
> —Booker T. Washington

If either one veers off track, other areas of your life suffer, too.

Let's take one last look at this chapter's profiled company. People choose UPS for its reputation, for the corporate persona that its neatly dressed and polite drivers represent, and for on-time package delivery. Why would people choose to know you or do business with you?

UPS delivers on its promises. Do you deliver on yours?

You will have successfully branded yourself when you align your self-impression with how others perceive you.

5. *Protect Your Financial Reputation (creditworthiness):*

How is this relevant to your reputation? Trust me, it is very relevant. Your financial reputation is represented by your credit report and it is often the first opportunity, and for some the only opportunity, to judge you. You have probably heard the saying "your reputation precedes you," and your credit report is a perfect example. Your credit report tells the world about your reputation for paying or not paying bills, your borrowing habits as well as your budgeting habits. In essence, it can be a tool to measure your growth pattern. It is also used as a tool to measure undesirable characteristics.

A company's credit reputation is a major factor in its ability to expand and grow. A company that is not financially sound will not attract investors and may have a problem obtaining the necessary bank financing to continue to grow and appropriately serve its customers or clients. If a company has poor credit, regardless of its stellar reputation to date, it will soon see an end to its existence. It is the same in our personal lives. Employers, schools, insurance companies, mortgage companies, car lots, credit card companies and other businesses, all look at our credit to determine our "trustworthiness." If trustworthiness is a characteristic that you value and want to be known for, a poor credit score can quickly ruin that brand. Therefore, your credit, and the reputation that it presumes, should be protected at all times.

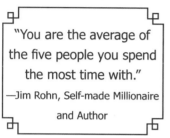

"You are the average of the five people you spend the most time with."

—Jim Rohn, Self-made Millionaire and Author

Just as important to your financial reputation is how you repay other businesses (people, friends). Bad news spreads fast. What's funny is that most times the person who is being talked about is the last one to hear the news.

Keeping your word in the respective communities you are a part of is a measure of your integrity. I've personally found that people who go back on their word to repay debts are just as untrustworthy in everything else that they do. They will steal if they think no one is watching, they will lie if they feel they can get away with it and they cheat on an ongoing basis. This cannot be you if you want to develop a positive brand for yourself and your family. Hold your brand to a high standard. Your brand, like you, has a personality!

The Family Brand

In addition to developing your own personal brand, you must influence your family brand and that of the people who are closest to you. That includes the reputation of your family as a whole and the individual members of your family.

My father used to say "you are a direct reflection of me." He said this whenever he thought my siblings and I were acting up or whenever any of us left the house. He reminded us who we represented – him – the family.

My father was right. Whenever I or my siblings did anything — good or bad — it was a reflection on my father. Our behavior either supported or damaged the brand that my father and mother had worked hard to develop for themselves as individuals, as a couple and for our family as a unit.

As you work on your personal branding, you must also consider your spouse and children. You are all reflections of each other. They must know your personal brand and they must support it. They support your brand by acting in ways that enhance your brand, not destroy it. However, your brand or desired brand must be communicated to them for them to effectively support it. They must also begin to develop their own personal brands that you can support.

> "In Prosperity Our Friends Know Us. In Adversity We Know Our friends. Never make someone a priority when you are only an option for them. If you are going to achieve excellence in big things, you develop the habit in little matters. Excellence is not an exception, it is a prevailing attitude."
> —Colin Powell
> American Statesman and Four Star General in the United States Army

Volunteering, covered in Key Principle #6, offers a great way for families to come together to solidify the family brand.

Social Media

Social media is growing and showing no signs of slowing. Facebook's membership alone has surpassed 550 million. Others such as Twitter, LinkedIn (primarily for business networking), MySpace and relative newcomers like Global14 all are experiencing stable or growing memberships. These social networking media provide the perfect opportunity to build your brand, or destroy it.

Building your brand takes years; unfortunately, destroying your brand can be accomplished in one click of the mouse.

Advantages

What are the advantages of using social media? It's simple to use and usually free of charge. It is relatively easy to set up an account and immediately start distributing information about yourself. Social media allows you to mobilize large numbers of people with little or no effort, time, or money.

You can easily manipulate social media to your advantage by using it as a platform for promoting your brand. For example, if you are seeking to declare yourself an expert in a particular area, start a blog that allows you to write and disseminate information that supports this knowledge. This effort may go a long way in helping you establish yourself as an expert. You can also use social media to gather information about others. And therein lies the problem.

Disadvantages

People tend to get emotionally engaged on social media sites. They make statements, share images and, in some cases, drop hints of future crimes to be committed. We all have to be on point when using this technology; this is your World Stage. I have told this to my son repeatedly. I explained to him that at the age of 22, Barack Obama had no idea that one day he would be considered a presidential hopeful, let alone become the president. I explained to my son that if 22-year-old Barack Obama had displayed some of the things he had done on his MySpace page, he would likely not be our president. We all have to remain thoughtful and careful; these modes of communication can be your best friend or your worst enemy. Always make smart business decisions when online!

Despite the immediacy and broad reach of social media, there is still no better way to tell the world about yourself than good old "boots on the ground." Nothing can replace a welcoming hand shake, a formal introduction, or face-to-face exchanges. Texting,

195

tweeting, and lurking in chat rooms provide anonymity for shy people and allow them to become even more introverted. These are poor business characteristics and you should be careful not to develop these habits.

Prosperous Life Advice on Social Media

Four Things to Always Remember About Social Media

1. **Discoverable** – Millions of people have access to otherwise personal or private information including thoughts and images.
2. **Subject to Interpretation** - The intent may not always be apparent and may be interpreted to your disadvantage.
3. **Editable** – Your information can be downloaded and edited to fit multiple purposes, some of which may not inure to your benefit.
4. **Eternal** – Information lasts forever in cyber space; positive or negative, good or bad.

Vision/Mission + Strengths/Weaknesses + Friends + Maintenance + Creditworthiness = **Brand**

Recommended reading:
http://www.fastcompany.com/magazine/10/brandyou.html?page=0%2C0

✑ Key Principle #9 ✑

Personal Image (Reputation)

Build an honorable personal and professional reputation.

Your reputation can make or break your business – and your personal relationships. It takes years to build and only seconds to destroy.

In The End...

I wrote this book to invoke a paradigm shift, a shift in the way you view your life, and to inspire you to take action towards making it better. Now that you have read Life is a Business! Manage It Better So You'll Enjoy It More, you have the basic concepts needed to make that happen. By understanding the 9 Key Principle s outlined in this book, and applying them to your life, you are almost assured a happier, more prosperous future. Now is the time to take action!

The other goal for writing this book was to develop, with the help of all of you, a mass movement, a movement that all who read this book would be inspired to participate in.

The Knowledge-Wealth-Prosperity Movement

The K.W.P. bus is rolling

This movement has no limits, and we are all expected to take part. I have customized a work book that can be purchased separately at www.charlesecoxjr.com/order. This work book will guide you through the process of organizing your life in more of a business structure, with the end goal of prosperity for all.

I have taken on the responsibility of leading, and participating in this movement. I will do all that it takes to deliver this message of "change" across North America, and beyond, through time tested methods, and new online platforms including: Webinars, Online Conferences, In Person Seminars, Blogging, Workshops, Tweets and Facebook just to name a few. From there I intend to move this message into corporate board rooms and classrooms across the country at every level. Who knows, there could one day be the "Prosperous Life Academy."

The Prosperous Life Movement has become near and dear to my heart. There's no reason why "we the people" should continue living as victims of the world's predators. Our prosperity is our responsibility.

The future of our country has been squarely placed on our shoulders. Fortunately for us we are blessed with tenacity, fortitude and broad shoulders.

I look forward to us working together to accomplish our goals. The sky is truly the limit.

Sincerely,

Charles E. Cox, Jr.

Will you live a life of prosperity?

Will you stop procrastinating and get your life going in the right direction?

The choice is yours, you have the tools.

Take action — today.

ABOUT THE AUTHOR

Charles E. Cox, Jr. is a native of Minnesota's Twin Cities. He is an author, speaker, philanthropist and serial entrepreneur with a passion for helping people of all ages and races find their inner strength through financial stability, entrepreneurism and overall financial literacy. Charles believes that the combination of a solid education with a deep understanding and respect for money will help all people on their journey to prosperity.

Charles' entrepreneurial spirit has led him to spend the last fifteen years of his career seeking challenging opportunities in real estate investment and sales, development and venture capitalism. Charles has also had careers in construction, including being a licensed general contractor and electrician in the state of Minnesota.

Charles also shares a deep commitment to youth development as well as strengthening all communities in which he participates.

Charles and his family currently reside in Minneapolis, Minnesota.

The Life Is A Business! Glossary of Terms

Acquisition – Something gained

Align – To get or fall in line

Assess – To determine the rate or amount of

Associations – An organization of persons having common interest

Budget – A plan for the coordination of resources and expenditures

Business – A particular field of endeavor; commercial or mercantile activity engaged in as a means of livelihood

Brand – To impress indelibly

CEO – Chief Executive Officer

CFO – Chief Financial Officer

COO – Chief Operations Officer

Coffer – Treasury; to store up in a coffer

Comparison – An examination of two or more items to establish similarities and differences

Contradict – To take issue with; say the opposite

Corporate Wellness Program – Offered by some employers as a combination of educational, organizational, and environmental activities designed to support behavior conducive to the health of employees in a business and their families

Credit – Belief or trust, confidence; the quality of being credible or trustworthy

Crisis – An emotionally significant event or radical change of status in a person's life; catastrophe

Declaration – The act of declaring; statement or announcement

Desire – To long or hope for; to express or wish for

Devise – To form in the mind by new combinations or applications of ideas or principles; formulate

Differentiate – To express the specific distinguishing quality of; to become distinct or different in character

Employer Identification Number (E.I.N.) – The corporate equivalent to a Social Security number

Empathy – The action of understanding, being aware of, being sensitive to the experience of another

Emulate – To strive to equal or match, especially by imitating

Endorphins – Proteins that function as neurotransmitters that reduce the sensation of pain and affect emotions

Enrich –To make rich or richer; to give greater value, importance, effectiveness

Euphoria – A feeling of vigor, well-being, or high spirits

Fiscal – Of or relating to financial matters

Fortune 500 Company – Refers to an annual listing compiled by Fortune magazine of the top 500 public companies in the U.S., as ranked by sales, assets, earnings, and capitalization.

Generation – The average span of time between the birth of parents and that of their offspring

Goodwill – An intangible asset which takes into account the value added to a business firm as a result of patronage, reputation, kindness, etc.

Guesstimate – An estimate made without adequate information; approximate calculation

Habitual – Doing, practicing, or acting in some manner by force of habit; routine, ongoing

Inception – An act, process, or instance of beginning

Impulse Buying – An unplanned decision to buy a product, just before purchase (emotions and feelings play a decisive role in purchasing, triggered by seeing the product or upon exposure to a well crafted promotional message)

Indulgence – The act of indulging oneself, or giving way to one's own desires

Inspiration – The act or power of moving the intellect or emotions; motivation, encouragement

Integrity – The firm adherence to an ethical code

Knowledge – The fact or condition of knowing something with familiarity gained through experience or association

Leader – A first or principal performer of a group; person in charge

Legacy – A gift by will, generally of money or other personal property or influence; anything handed down from, or as from, an ancestor

Manifest – Make evident or certain by showing or displaying; reveal

Mannerism – A characteristic, and often unconscious, mode of action

Mission – A specific task with which a person or a group is charged; vocation or purpose

Movement – The act or process of moving; especially: change of place or position or posture

Negative – Lacking positive qualities; damaging

Outline – A summary of a written work

Philanthropy – An active effort to promote human welfare; benevolence

Positive – Fully assured; certain

Predator – One that preys, destroys, or devours

Predetermined – To impose a direction or tendency on beforehand; fated

Preparedness – A state of adequate preparation "in case of readiness"

Proactive – Acting in anticipation of future problems, needs, or changes

Process – A series of actions or operations conducing to an end

Procrastinate – To put off intentionally or habitually; postpone

Productivity – The quality or state of being productive; output

Prosperity – The state of flourishing, thriving, success, or good fortune

Realistic – Concern or fact or reality; pragmatic

Reputation – Overall quality or character as seen or judged by people in general

Responsibility – Reliability, trustworthiness

Rigorous – Very strict; demanding

Social Responsibility – An ethical ideology that an entity has an obligation to act to benefit society at large

Social Security Number – A number that's issued by the Internal Revenue Service (IRS); primary function is to track individuals for taxation purposes

Stakeholder – A person entrusted with the stakes of; a person affected by the decisions of an entity

Stewardship – The conducting, supervising, or managing of something; the careful and responsible management of something entrusted to one's care

Structure – Something arranged in a definite pattern or organization

Sustainability – Of or relating to a lifestyle involving the use of sustainable methods; maintaining

S.W.O.T. Analysis (Strengths, Weaknesses, Opportunities, Threats) – A corporately popular strategic planning method involved in a business venture or project

Tax Identification Number (T.I.N.) – Identifying number for tax purposes

Vision – Mode of seeing or conceiving; the act or power of imagination; foresight

Volunteer – An unpaid helper; to offer oneself as a volunteer

Vulnerable – Open to attack or damage; defenseless

Wealth – The condition of being successful or thriving; especially: economic well-being

Wellness – The quality or state of being in good health as an actively sought goal

Wholeheartedly – Completely or sincerely devoted, determined, or enthusiastic; unconditionally

Wherewithal – Means, resources, money

Purchase your Life Is A Business! products at
www.charlesecoxjr.com/order

Buy The Workbook
Coming in 2012!

Buy The Hardback
$29.99

Buy The Paperback
$19.99

Buy The eBook
$9.99

Buy The CD Set
$14.99